I0559344

FENIX TV
INTRODUCES

THE
VOICES OF
100
WOMEN

A GROUNDBREAKING BOOK
FEATURING WOMEN
FROM ALL AROUND THE WORLD

HANNA OLIVAS AND **ADRIANA LUNA CARLOS**
ALONG WITH 20 INSPIRING AUTHORS

© 2024 ALL RIGHTS RESERVED.

Published by She Rises Studios Publishing **www.SheRisesStudios.com**.

No part of this book may be reproduced or transmitted in any form whatsoever, electronic, or mechanical, including photocopying, recording, or by any informational storage or retrieval system without the expressed written, dated and signed permission from the publisher and co-authors.

LIMITS OF LIABILITY/DISCLAIMER OF WARRANTY:

The co-authors and publisher of this book have used their best efforts in preparing this material. While every attempt has been made to verify the information provided in this book, neither the co-authors nor the publisher assumes any responsibility for any errors, omissions, or inaccuracies.

The co-authors and publisher make no representation or warranties with respect to the accuracy, applicability, or completeness of the contents of this book. They disclaim any warranties (expressed or implied), merchantability, or for any purpose. The co-authors and publisher shall in no event be held liable for any loss or other damages, including but not limited to special, incidental, consequential, or other damages.

ISBN: 978-1-964619-52-1

TABLE OF CONTENTS

INTRODUCTION

Welcome to **The Voices of 100 Women - Volume 1**, an anthology that invites you to embark on a transformative journey through the diverse and powerful narratives of women from around the globe. In this collection, the first 22 of the 100 remarkable voices will share their unique stories of resilience, strength, and triumph, celebrating their myriad experiences.

In these pages, you will find a rich tapestry woven from the threads of personal essays, interviews, and reflective pieces. Each contribution offers an intimate glimpse into the lives of women who are trailblazers, caregivers, innovators, and everyday heroes. From the groundbreaking achievements of those who challenge the status quo to the quiet courage of women navigating their individual challenges, this anthology reflects the universal yet deeply personal facets of womanhood.

As you explore the themes of empowerment, identity, and solidarity, you will encounter stories that resonate across cultures and continents, highlighting the shared struggles and triumphs that unite us all. This collection captures the essence of women's lived experiences, reminding us that every voice matters and contributes to a larger conversation about equality and strength.

The Voices of 100 Women is more than just a book—it's a call to action, an invitation to listen, learn, and engage with the powerful stories that shape our world. As you turn the pages, may you find inspiration in these narratives and feel the heartbeat of a movement that celebrates women everywhere. Welcome to a celebration of voices—welcome to a celebration of you.

Hanna Olivas

Founder and CEO of SHE RISES STUDIOS

https://www.linkedin.com/company/she-rises-studios/
https://www.facebook.com/sherisesstudios
https://www.instagram.com/sherisesstudios_llc/
www.SheRisesStudios.com

Author, Speaker, and Founder. Hanna was born and raised in Las Vegas, Nevada, and has paved her way to becoming one of the most influential women of 2022. Hanna is the co-founder of She Rises Studios and the founder of the Brave & Beautiful Blood Cancer Foundation. Her journey started in 2017 when she was first diagnosed with Multiple Myeloma, an incurable blood cancer. Now more than ever, her focus is to empower other women to become leaders because The Future is Female. She is currently traveling and speaking publicly to women to educate them on entrepreneurship, leadership, and owning the female power within.

The Power of Women's Voices: Rising, Inspiring, and Unstoppable

By Hanna Olivas

From every corner of the world, across different cultures, languages, and backgrounds, there is a common thread that weaves through the lives of women—their voices. These voices, often stifled or dismissed, carry within them the power to ignite change, spark inspiration, and shift the tides of history. Yet, too often, they go unheard. The world is rich with the untold stories of women who have overcome adversity, shattered expectations, and redefined what it means to be powerful.

This chapter is not just about the act of speaking—it is about the deeper significance of why women's voices are so essential in our world today. It is about how these voices, once unleashed, have the power to transform lives, communities, and societies. And it is about why, now more than ever, we must listen, we must amplify, and we must celebrate the voices of women from around the globe.

The voices of women have always been a source of strength, though in many parts of the world, they were silenced by patriarchal norms or systemic inequalities. But there has always been a flame burning deep within, a desire to be heard, to be understood, and to be valued. For centuries, women's stories were told for them—by men, by institutions, by cultures that sought to define who they should be. But in the quiet corners of kitchens, in the intimate conversations among friends, and in the hearts of those who dared to dream, the voices of women never disappeared. They simply waited for the right moment to rise.

And rise they did.

One by one, across continents and generations, women have begun to reclaim their voices. From the boardrooms of corporate America to the rural villages of Africa, from the bustling streets of Europe to the highlands of South America, women are stepping forward, not just to speak, but to be heard. And in that hearing, they are inspiring others to rise with them.

It's in the act of listening that we create true connections. Listening builds bridges of understanding, allowing us to step into the shoes of another and truly grasp the weight of her journey. Listening allows us to share in the victories and the struggles of those who walk paths different from our own, and it is through this shared understanding that we realize the vastness of our collective strength.

I think of Nadia, a woman from Egypt, whose story exemplifies the power of this transformation. Growing up in a conservative household, she was taught that a woman's silence was her virtue. Her grandmother, a devout woman, would say, "A quiet woman is a virtuous woman." For much of her life, Nadia abided by this rule. She kept her thoughts to herself, tucked away her dreams, and allowed the men around her to dominate the conversation. But deep inside, she longed to be free, to express the thoughts and ideas that swirled inside her.

It wasn't until she attended a women's conference, where women from across the globe shared their stories, that something inside her shifted. She was captivated by the courage of the women who spoke. They were bold, fearless, and unapologetic. Each woman's story was unique, yet there was a common thread of resilience, strength, and determination. As she listened to them, Nadia realized that silence was not her power—her voice was. "I realized that I wasn't meant to stay quiet," she said. "I had a voice, and it was meant to be heard."

Today, Nadia is a fierce advocate for women's rights in her community. She uses her platform to challenge the norms that once kept her silent, and in doing so, she inspires other women to rise and speak their truths. Her journey from silence to speaking out reflects the experiences of countless women around the world who are reclaiming their voices and refusing to be silenced any longer.

These voices, once freed, carry the weight of generations. They are not just stories of individual triumph—they are stories of collective power. When one woman speaks her truth, she gives permission to others to do the same. And this creates a ripple effect, spreading far beyond the initial conversation, touching lives in ways we may never fully understand. Every time a woman speaks, she breaks the chains of silence for herself and for those who come after her.

But this chapter is not just about celebrating the triumphs. It is about recognizing the challenges that come with stepping into our power. It's about the fears and doubts that often accompany the decision to live authentically and speak our truths. For every woman who has found her voice, there are many others still searching for theirs. The voices in their heads, the doubts, the fears—they all whisper, telling them that they're not enough, that their stories don't matter.

Lila, a woman from Mexico, shared with me her battle with imposter syndrome. Despite her success in business, she constantly felt like she didn't deserve her achievements. "I would walk into boardrooms filled with men, and I felt like a fraud," Lila told me. "No matter how much I accomplished, there was always this voice inside me telling me I didn't belong."

Lila's story is not unique. So many women, especially those in male-dominated fields, have felt the pressure to prove themselves. They feel the weight of needing to be twice as good just to be seen as equal. The internal battle can be exhausting, and it's easy to believe that we are alone in these struggles. But through the stories of others, Lila found comfort and validation. "When I started hearing other women share similar experiences, I realized that I wasn't alone. So many successful women had felt the same way at some point. And that realization helped me start to silence those negative voices."

Now, Lila mentors young women entering the business world. She tells them, "Your seat at the table is earned. Don't let anyone, including yourself, tell you otherwise." She helps them navigate the challenges of imposter syndrome, encouraging them to own their success and speak their truths. Her story is a powerful reminder that the more we share our experiences, the more we help others rise above their doubts and fears.

As we listen to these stories, one theme continues to emerge: the importance of self-love and self-compassion. So many of the women I've spoken with have shared stories of learning to love themselves after years of self-doubt, criticism, and shame. The journey to self-love is not always an easy one, but it is essential to living a life of authenticity and empowerment.

Sofia, a woman from Italy, talked about her struggle with body image and self-worth. For years, she internalized the messages she received from the media, from her family, and from society at large that told her she wasn't enough. "I spent most of my life trying to change myself to fit into some ideal that I thought would make me worthy of love," Sofia shared. "I was constantly dieting, constantly criticizing myself, constantly feeling like I was never enough."

It wasn't until Sofia attended a women's retreat, where the focus was on self-love and body acceptance, that she began to shift her perspective. Surrounded by women who were embracing themselves fully—flaws and all—Sofia began to see herself through a new lens. "I realized that my worth wasn't tied to how I looked. My worth was inherent, simply because I existed."

Sofia's journey to self-love was a gradual one, filled with ups and downs, but today she is a vocal advocate for body positivity and self-acceptance. She uses her platform to encourage other women to embrace themselves fully and unapologetically. "Loving yourself is a radical act," Sofia told me. "It's an act of defiance in a world that constantly tells women they're not enough. But when you choose to love yourself, you reclaim your power."

The voices of women are powerful not only because they inspire change in others, but because they reflect the strength and resilience that lies within each of us. They remind us that, no matter where we come from or what we've experienced, we are capable of rising above our circumstances and creating the life we desire.

As I continued to gather stories from women around the world, one thing became increasingly clear: the power of women's voices does not lie in their volume or in the grandeur of their words. It lies in their authenticity, in their willingness to share their truth, even when it is difficult, even when it is uncomfortable. It lies in their ability to connect with others on a deeper level, to create a space where vulnerability and courage can coexist.

These voices remind us that we are not alone in our struggles. They remind us that we are part of something much bigger than ourselves— a global sisterhood of women who are rising together, lifting each other up, and creating a future where every woman can thrive.

As I reflect on the stories of these women, I am filled with awe at the incredible strength, resilience, and wisdom that exists within each of us. These women have faced unimaginable challenges, yet they have risen above them with grace and courage. They have refused to be defined by their circumstances, instead choosing to define themselves on their own terms.

And in doing so, they have created a powerful legacy—not just for themselves, but for all of us. Their stories remind us that our struggles do not diminish us, but strengthen us. They remind us that we have the power to shape our own destinies, to create the lives we desire, and to inspire others to do the same.

As we continue to share our stories, we build a world where every woman's voice is valued, where every woman's experience is honored, and where every woman's potential is realized. We create a world where collaboration replaces competition, where love replaces fear, and where unity replaces division.

This is the power of our voices.

Adriana Luna Carlos

Founder and CEO of SHE RISES STUDIOS & FENIX TV

https://www.linkedin.com/in/adriana-luna-carlos/
https://www.facebook.com/adrianalunacarlos
https://www.instagram.com/sherisesstudios_llc/
https://www.sherisesstudios.com/
https://fenixtv.app/

Adriana Luna Carlos is an accomplished web and graphic designer, author, and mentor with a passion for helping women succeed in life and business. With over 10 years of experience in graphic and web arts, Adriana has built a reputation as an innovative leader and entrepreneur. In 2020, she co-founded She Rises Studios, a multi-digital media company and publishing house that has helped countless clients achieve their branding and marketing goals. In 2023, she co-created FENIX TV, an online streaming platform that showcases stories of people breaking barriers, shattering stereotypes, and triumphing against the odds.

As an advocate for women's success, Adriana challenges her clients and mentees to strive for nothing less than excellence. She has a deep understanding of the insecurities and challenges that women often face in the business world and provides the guidance and resources needed to overcome them. Her success as a business leader and entrepreneur has made her a sought-after mentor and speaker at events around the world.

Through her work, Adriana has demonstrated a commitment to creating opportunities for women to succeed in business and life. Her passion for innovation, leadership, and women's empowerment has made her a respected figure in the business community, and her impact will undoubtedly continue to inspire and empower women for years to come.

The Power of Our Voices

By Adriana Luna Carlos

In every journey, there comes a moment when we realize that the strength we need to move forward has always been within us. For me, that moment didn't arrive in a single grand revelation, but through a series of small, significant experiences that shaped my understanding of self-worth, resilience, and what it means to rise above life's challenges.

I come from a family who truly values the worth of hard work. We say what we mean, and we do what we say. My path wasn't just about following in the footsteps of those before me. It was about carving my own way, even when I felt unsure, insecure, or small. The beauty of my journey has been the realization that, as women, we are capable of much more than we give ourselves credit for. The real magic happens when we start believing in our own potential.

Growing up, I didn't always feel like I had a voice. I was surrounded by strong, opinionated family members, but I wasn't always sure where I fit in. I thrived in school and loved helping others, yet I often forgot to extend that same care to myself. Over time, I accepted toxic traits from others, excused behavior I shouldn't have, and slowly, my self-worth began to erode.

For years, I struggled with confidence, doubting myself and my abilities. It wasn't until a toxic relationship forced me to confront the reality of how much I had diminished myself that I began the hard work of rediscovering who I was. Leaving that relationship was one of the most difficult decisions I've ever made, but it was also the beginning of a new chapter in my life—the chapter where I finally started to find my voice.

I learned that reclaiming your voice isn't about being the loudest or most assertive person in the room. It's about listening to yourself, trusting your instincts, and knowing that your perspective matters. Finding my voice wasn't just about speaking up; it was about understanding that I had something valuable to contribute, that my story—my experiences—had the power to inspire others.

Every journey has its obstacles, and mine was no exception. As I started to rebuild my confidence, I also began to dream bigger. But with big dreams come big challenges. Running a business at a young age wasn't easy. I faced financial struggles, learned how to juggle multiple responsibilities, and had to teach myself how to navigate a world that wasn't always welcoming to young women in leadership.

One of the most challenging aspects was learning how to balance my personal life with my growing ambitions. There were times when I felt like I was failing at both—struggling to keep up with client demands while also trying to maintain friendships and relationships. But over time, I learned that balance isn't something you achieve once and for all. It's something you continually work at. And that's okay.

The real lesson came in understanding that the challenges I faced weren't signs of failure—they were opportunities to grow. They taught me resilience. They reminded me that success isn't about never stumbling; it's about how you rise after you fall. Every setback became a lesson, and every challenge a stepping stone to something greater.

One of the most powerful things I've learned along the way is the importance of community. We don't have to do this alone. Whether we're building a business, raising a family, or simply navigating the ups and downs of life, having a support system can make all the difference.

That's one of the reasons I co-founded She Rises Studios. I wanted to create a space where women could come together, support one another, and feel empowered to pursue their dreams without fear. So often, we're taught to compete, to see other women as our rivals. But in my experience, there's nothing more powerful than women lifting each other up.

In the communities I've built, both in business and in my personal life, I've found strength I didn't know I had. I've learned that when we share our stories, we create space for others to share theirs. And in that sharing, we find healing, inspiration, and the courage to keep going.

There's something incredibly powerful about owning your story. For a long time, I didn't want to look back at the difficult moments in my life. I wanted to forget the struggles, the failures, the pain. But I've come to realize that those experiences are part of who I am. They don't define me, but they have shaped me.

When I look back now, I see a woman who has faced adversity and come out stronger on the other side. I see someone who has learned to trust herself, to believe in her own worth, and to embrace the power of her voice. I see someone who, despite the setbacks, has continued to dream big and work toward a future where other women can do the same.

Our stories, no matter how difficult or painful, have the power to inspire others. When we share our experiences, we give others permission to do the same. We remind them that they are not alone, that they too can rise above whatever challenges they're facing. And in doing so, we create a ripple effect—one that empowers not just ourselves, but the women around us.

If there's one thing I've learned through all of this, it's that dreams are never static. They evolve as we do. The dreams I had when I started out are not the same as the dreams I hold today. They've grown, shifted, and changed alongside me. And that's the beauty of it.

Today, my dream is to continue building spaces where women feel empowered to pursue their passions. Whether it's through She Rises

Studios, my design work, or simply through the conversations I have with other women, I want to be a source of support, inspiration, and empowerment.

As I continue to move forward, I'm constantly reminded of how far I've come—and how far I still have to go. But instead of feeling overwhelmed by the distance, I'm excited. I know that every step I take brings me closer to the woman I'm becoming, and that every challenge I face is an opportunity for growth.

At the end of the day, my story is just one of many. But what I've learned is that every woman's voice matters. Every woman's journey is unique, but there are threads that connect us all—strength, resilience, hope, and the power to rise above.

My hope is that by sharing my story, I can inspire others to embrace theirs. To believe in their own worth, to pursue their dreams, and to know that they have the power to create the life they want. We all have challenges, but we also have the strength to overcome them. And when we come together, when we support each other, there's nothing we can't achieve.

So, to all the women reading this, I want to leave you with this: Don't be afraid to dream big. Don't be afraid to rise. Your voice matters, your story matters, and the world needs what only you can offer. Together, we can create a future where every woman is empowered to be her fullest, most authentic self. Together, we rise.

Sylvia Becker-Hill

Founder of Becker-Hill Inc.

https://www.linkedin.com/in/sylviabeckerhill/
https://www.facebook.com/SylviaBeckerHillBiz
https://www.instagram.com/sylviabeckerhill/
https://becker-hill.com/
https://talkwithsylvia.com/

Sylvia Becker-Hill is a true Renaissance woman, a 9-times published bestselling author, and a seasoned edutainer who has empowered thousands of corporate executives, women leaders, and entrepreneurs around the world since 1997.

In 2002, she became the first German coach to earn the coveted title of Professional Certified Coach from the International Coach Federation, establishing herself as an industry-shaping pioneer in the coaching world.

Her impressive educational background boasts two university degrees, while her portfolio showcases over 30 certifications in various change modalities, including her accreditation as one of the world's first 10 Certified Master Neuroplasticians in 2023.

Sylvia's mission is to empower you with all the knowledge, tools, and lasting transformation you need to "FLIP" everything that bothers, hurts, or blocks you from living your dream life into unquestionable Freedom, unconditional Love, envisioned Identity, and impactful Power.

Are you ready to feel unabashedly alive and powerful?

Crazy, Courage, Charisma

By Sylvia Becker-Hill

FLIP Inherited Trauma Into Triumph

"I always felt like a bird without wings,
Meant to soar yet drowning in thoughts and things.
Books as friends, food for comfort, clothes as protective masks…
Why did no one ever ask:
Why are you truly here?
What do you hold dear?"
—Sylvia Becker-Hill

"Sometimes a breakdown can be the beginning of a kind of
breakthrough, a way of living in advance through a trauma
that prepares you for a future of radical transformation."
—Cherrie Moraga

Just a few weeks before my 57th birthday, after what I considered one of the best years of my life, my body tried to kill me. It was a total shock. I hadn't seen it coming.

Sure, I was overweight with high blood pressure and cholesterol, but I felt great and was addressing it. I did Pilates and yoga, walked, ate healthily, drank minimal coffee and alcohol, and avoided sugar. I took loads of supplements. In my eyes, I was healthier than most and doing everything right.

Yet, there I was: in the ER, rescued by six hunky paramedics who stormed our house after my husband Peter called 911 because I couldn't breathe. I stayed calm, hearing my "angel voice" saying: "Don't worry, Darling, you are not going to die tonight." Peter knew I'd be fine when he saw me joking with the fire department guys carrying me into the ambulance. They quickly injected a huge dose of Benadryl into my arm to reduce the windpipe swelling so I could breathe again.

After my body's betrayal and the medical establishment offering no explanations, just pharmaceuticals to suppress symptoms, **I fully said "yes" to myself, my body, my health, and my truth.**

I stopped working and dedicated my time and savings to figuring out why my body turned against me.

What had I been blind to? What was going on inside me?

I didn't fully understand it yet. Part of my self-healing journey was to become a full-time writer—emphasis on "writer." I had been a published author multiple times over the past 20 years, but those books were just marketing tools for my executive coaching business. They aimed to empower other women with edgy information and new coaching processes. They weren't about me. Writing was only a sporadic activity, a means to an end, teaching ideas and concepts from a lifetime of research. It wasn't a form of self-expression to clarify my own beliefs and worldviews. It wasn't about healing myself.

Now, writing changed for me. It is deeply intimate, raw, and honest between myself, the observer, and my various parts: my subconscious and conscious mind, my soul and human self, my mind and body, my heart and yours. Will these parts understand each other?

Can I write myself into aliveness, wholeness, belonging, peace, and freedom?

Will you understand and stick with me to the end?

I'm terrified you won't. I fear my writing is terrible, that I'll perpetuate my childhood experience of "no one understands me," and that I'll pour out my deepest feelings and repel or bore you. I could handle it if you didn't understand my sometimes strange, abstract thoughts, but I would be devastated if I bored you. Writing boringly would mean I wasted your time and attention, and that, to me, is a big sin. Life is too precious.

Life feels like a miracle to me, every moment is filled with magic. Wasting time in boredom, oblivion, ignorance, or apathy is a waste of human potential. There's no bigger pain in my eyes. I face it almost daily when I go to bed and my incessant mind points to the gap between my big vision and the meager approximation of my day's results. My warrior heart loves me despite my daily failings in the eyes of my "picture-perfect, perfectionistic, uber-educated mind."

Are you still with me? Or did I lose you already? With my rambling thoughts faster than my hand could write?

I'm still at the beginning, trying to tell you what my solo book in the 100 Voices of Women series is all about, offering you a summary, a glimpse here in this chapter. But despite having written many executive summaries in the past, I refuse to write another perfect, polished professional like those here. **I want to write in a way that satisfies my longing to come home within myself, hoping that in doing so, it will inspire you to come home within yourself too.** That's why I'm trying a different style here: messy, meandering, the real me pouring onto these pages while being in my body and sensing more than thinking what wants to be written out of me.

Hello? Are you still there?

I want to share moments when I truly felt I was going crazy. I want to develop with you a deeper understanding of what "crazy" even means and how we all experience it sometimes. Maybe even daily...

Before I define it, stop for a moment and consider: **When in your life have you felt "going crazy"?** And how would you define that experience in your own words?

Defining "Going Crazy"

"Being conscious of one's own insanity is simply inner hell.
Ignorance can seem like an unattainable yet alluring escape."
—*Sylvia Becker-Hill*

When you google definitions of "crazy," you'll find they refer to abnormal mental states or out-of-control behavior. For example, Psychology Today defines psychosis as "the presence of delusions, hallucinations, and disorganization of thought and speech." Merriam-Webster Dictionary defines acting crazy as "to act in a way that is out of control: to act wildly."

For me, it was **a secret inner turmoil I tried to hide.** A state of inner fragility, as if my body was trembling inside, combined with childlike anxiety about an unknown looming just beyond my perception, topped by frustration at not controlling my feelings and actions. In short: When my subconscious mind takes over and I watch myself do things I consciously don't want to do, I feel like I'm going crazy. Or even simpler: **I feel crazy when I can't control myself.**

Here's a simple example. It might seem trivial, but for me, it's a huge inner battle between willpower and deeply ingrained old subconscious coping mechanisms!

I'm educated as a Certified Master Neuroplastician and know the importance of good quality sleep for my well-being. I know my best bedtime routine: going to bed before 10 pm and winding down without blue light from any screens helps me fall asleep easily. I know that! I promise myself not to watch late TV or scroll mindlessly on my phone in bed…

But then: I watch a TV episode and get hooked on the cliffhanger, promising myself "just 10 minutes of the next episode," and two or three episodes later, nearly falling asleep on the sofa I go to bed way too late, only to end up scrolling through Facebook for 45 minutes while my husband snores beside me.

This isn't a once-a-month event. It's a five-day-a-week occurrence. As a powerful executive coach for nearly 28 years, who easily empowers others to break bad habits and form healthy ones, it's beyond frustrating to be a powerless puppet on the strings of my subconscious mind!

I've tried everything—from living without a TV to expensive coaching with habit experts, deep hypnosis, and past life regression. Being consciously committed and 100% present to my self-sabotage, but not being able to stop my actions, is my definition of "crazy." This is not a judgemental label I give myself. It is an inner tangible somatic takeover of disturbing scary somatic sensations, a full-body hell and not mean self-talk!

Before I share more "episodes of crazy" and how to overcome them and heal ourselves, stop again, breathe, and consider: Can you relate to what I shared? **Do you see patterns in your life where you act subconsciously pulled against your conscious goals and commitments?** Can you emotionally relate to why this feels like "going crazy" to me?

Early Childhood Prophecy

"The younger we were, the more impressionable our brains.
What adults we believed in told us was branded as truth into
our neurocircuits,
like a rancher's initials seared into a cattle's hide."
—Sylvia Becker-Hill

I remember it well, even though it happened over 53 years ago. It is my second oldest significant memory. I was between 3 and 4 years old and had been in kindergarten for a few months (In Germany, we go to kindergarten before preschool). My kindergarten teacher had invited my parents and me to a special meeting. I sadly forgot her name and don't remember her face or clothes, but I remember the setup, the furniture, her voice, and me sitting between my parents. We three sat on too-small-for-adults kids' chairs opposite the higher desk of my kindergarten teacher, who sat on her big adult chair. The setup gave her the aura of a judge holding court. I still remember how embarrassed my dad was, trying to balance his big heavy body on that tiny chair!

My kindergarten teacher showed my parents a drawing I had made with crayons. It showed a tree, grass, flowers, a big smiling sun, a house, my parents, and me as simple figures. It looked normal to me, and I wondered why my parents were summoned and if I had made a mistake. Indeed, **something was wrong**, but I didn't get punished; I got praised! My kindergarten teacher pointed with her long index finger to some lines I had drawn to place the house in relation to the tree and sun and said in her authoritative "judge" voice: "This is NOT how a normal 3-year-old's brain usually draws! This is a three-dimensional perspective drawing that even many adults get wrong! **Your daughter is very special. She's going to go very far.**"

She didn't know that what she meant as a compliment and encouragement would turn into something horrible for me. My parents, whose childhoods were destroyed by World War II and traumatic experiences leaving them with PTSD and little education, were simple people. Naturally, they were proud of what my kindergarten teacher said and repeated her words at parties, to relatives and neighbors. Yet, they didn't know what to do with it and me! Concepts like "the gifted child" or "neurodiverse" didn't exist in Germany then. Neither my parents nor any other teacher had the insight or resources to understand and manage my "unusual mind."

Instead of feeling empowered, I felt doomed. Those words from my kindergarten teacher didn't gift me confidence or become a meme of proudly claimed identity. No, those words felt like a prophecy of doom, leading to decades of **heartbreaking loneliness as an outcast among my peers.** Worse, it became a curse I resisted and fought against while also embracing and longing to fulfill. This ambivalence led to a lifelong battle with a **persistent sense of failure** because I could neither "blend in" nor reach the success prophesied for me. This battle was utterly exhausting. I believed I was going crazy, with a goal-point of success on the horizon always moving further out of reach just when I thought I could nearly touch it. Like a donkey's carrot on a stick that teases and entices him yet is designed to stay out of reach to keep him moving.

I hadn't thought about this memory in years, but after my body tried to kill me, it resurfaced as an important puzzle piece to understand how I created the chronic yet invisible stress that led to my body's breaking point.

What prophecies did you hear as a young child that created strong patterns in your life, weaving like threads of a tapestry to form a distinct image—some beautiful, some ugly, some wanted, some unwanted? **Were there any sentences or memes that made you "go crazy" later?**

The Power of Trauma or
How Our Stories Reside in Our Bodies

"When all you know is fight or flight, red flags, and butterflies all feel the same."
—*Cindy Cherie, Australian Poet*

"The essence of trauma is disconnection from ourselves. Trauma is not terrible things that happen from the other side—those are traumatic. But the trauma is that very separation from the body and emotions."
—*Gabor Mate, Canadian Physician*

Thanks to groundbreaking research and Bessel van der Kolk's bestseller *The Body Keeps the Score* from 2015, along with insights from other somatic experts shared, we now understand several crucial aspects of trauma:

1. Trauma isn't solely defined by external events like war or abuse but by our **overwhelmed brain and body's internal reaction** to any intensely emotional experience our immature brains as children struggle to process at the time.

2. The triggering event **can be seemingly minor to others, yet profoundly impactful** to the individual—such as enduring discomfort in a dirty diaper as an infant.

3. Trauma is a **universal human experience**, varying in intensity and prevalence across individuals.

4. **Trauma lodges itself on a cellular level within our bodies.**

5. Talkin and intellectual understanding alone rarely suffice to fully heal trauma; **somatic approaches are essential to release trapped energy.**

6. **Unreleased trauma can accumulate**, leading to chronic stress and inflammation, often resulting in physical ailments.

7. **Trauma can be inherited** genetically or absorbed through societal and cultural influences and the collective field.

My memoir-style book explores how I navigated and healed family and collective traumas unknowingly carried in my body for most of my life.

What was your perception of trauma before reading this chapter? Did these seven points summarizing two decades of research provide new insights? **How do you identify traumas influencing your life?**

The Gift of Courage or Life as a Dandelion

"Dandelions are like me:

Growing in hostile places, seen as weed...
Yet in truth, they're like a heroine,
Bringing hope to those in need,
Blowing down walls of their 'inner Berlin'."
—Sylvia Becker-Hill

"Most people go through life dreading they'll have a traumatic
experience.
Freaks were born with their trauma.
They've already passed their test in life.
They're aristocrats."
—Diane Arbus, American Photographer

In the fall of 2012, I stood in my windowless bathroom off the master bedroom in our picturesque house in Michigan, complete with red shutters and a charming white picket fence. My husband and boys were gone, leaving the house eerily quiet. Yet, the keyword here is "windowless." I was entirely alone in a confined space but felt mentally and physically restless. Suddenly, a strong sensation washed over me— I felt both watched and judged, bombarded by a relentless stream of constant comments. It was deafening as if hundreds of people were shouting at me through loudspeakers and megaphones, filling the small bathroom.

Then, I realized with shock that this cacophony of noise was all in my own mind. And **it had been there my entire life...**

I had never truly been alone, never free from this intrusive commentary, even in my most private moments. It was surreal. Amidst this torrent of judgments, the most persistent thought was: "WHAT WILL THE NEIGHBORS THINK?" Yet, it wasn't just our real neighbors; it was my family, parents, grandparents, friends, clients, Germans from both present and past—Stasi, Nazis, the German government—all echoing their expectations and rules.

I recognized this pervasive sense of judgment as deeply rooted in German cultural norms, where scrutiny and conformity ensure safety and protect families. These judgments echoed endlessly in my mind like a broken record, **an inner hell of perpetual inadequacy** despite the seemingly perfect life my husband and I had built.

I didn't know at the time that I was becoming aware of inherited trauma from my family and the collective subconsciousness of Germans. Nonetheless, using the Emotional Freedom Technique—EFT also known as "tapping"—I emotionally felt through it all and released stuck energy from my body with tears and physical shaking. **I have been free of these tormenting commentaries that haunted me for most of my life for over 12 years now!**

It took courage not to flee the bathroom at the first sound of those voices, not to turn on the TV for distraction, or to seek solace in the kitchen with food. Instead, it took courage to remain amidst the storm, confront it, and guide me through the release process with a transformative tool. I am still proud of that moment. It felt like living through a horror movie and vanquishing the demon, except it was real and not Hollywood fantasy.

Looking back, I understand better what I did back then: **I turned trauma into triumph by facing, feeling, and releasing it.**

This is my message for you:

No matter how daunting or terrifying something may seem, the fact that you have made it this far in life means **you have the brain and body capacity to face it, feel it—without losing yourself—and release it for good.** I know it's not easy. Not all stories in my book transform traumas as swiftly as this one did. Sometimes it's arduous and requires repetition and professional support. But the key point is: **It is possible.** You can eventually reach that point of freedom **as long as you resist the urge to flee, distract, or numb yourself.**

I chose the dandelion as a symbol of the courage I discovered because, despite its reputation as a weed, **the dandelion is a resilient flower.** Often found along roadsides, near dumpsters, and amid cracked asphalt, it always turns its glowing yellow face toward the sun, embracing life fully despite sometimes being trampled or driven over. As it ages, it proudly spreads its seeds, offering free wishes to all, trusting that its seeds will find fertile ground and sprout new life.

For everyone who holds their head high despite adversity and the scars of trauma, **we are like dandelions: Beautiful, resilient, and filled with magic!**

Keep reaching for the sun and allow the seeds of your efforts to find fertile soil.

In the end, my kindergarten teacher was right: I have come very far, farther than any of my beloved family members who came before me...

Molly Smith

Next Best Step, LLC.
Chief Positivity Officer

https://www.linkedin.com/in/molly-smith-24345712/
https://www.facebook.com/molly.m.smith.90
https://www.instagram.com/molly.positivepants/
https://nextbeststep.co/

Having been described as the female "Ted Lasso", Molly approaches life with a combination of grit and positivity... hence her personal moniker #mollypositivepants. She is deeply committed to her own personal growth, the potential of the people around her, and the success of the companies she leads.

In March of 2019, she made a game-changing decision that altered the trajectory of her life: she decided to finally focus on her health. While gaining alignment in her health, Molly was awakened to the possibility that helping others overcome the obstacles that she's tackled is the key to impacting thousands of people using her unique, quirky brand of self-deprecating humor.

Molly is the founder and Chief Positivity Officer of Next Best Step LLC, a company dedicated to helping others take their next best step in their health, mindset and purpose.

Getting Out of the Funk

By Molly Smith

In March of 2023, during a conversation with my boss, I uttered what felt like the single scariest sentence of my adult life:

"If success in this role is going to require me to spend 50% or more of my time talking to large foundations and national nonprofits, then I don't think I'm the right person for this role."

It was a moment of raw vulnerability, and I had to muster all my strength to keep my composure.

Despite holding a C-level position for the previous three years, I found myself in a career funk. My core skills and experience were no longer aligned with how my job responsibilities were evolving. I'm the kind of person and leader who rolls up their sleeves, tackles challenges head-on, and gets things done, but where the role was going was further away from my giftedness. The previous 25+ years of my career had been in software and technology operations, not nonprofit business development which is a very different skill set.

Over the previous 6–8 months, as discussions about the need to cultivate partnerships in the nonprofit sector intensified, so did my imposter syndrome. The weight of trying to fill this gap became increasingly more difficult, which left me feeling utterly miserable. In an attempt to find solace, I focused on the aspects of my job where I excelled—operations management, process creation and optimization, and team development. These were the areas where I felt fulfilled and added the most value to the company.

Yet, on the days when I found myself trying to make inroads with national nonprofits and foundations, my feelings of inadequacy became a daily struggle. I coped by escaping and numbing those emotions with the daily glass or three of wine, opening whatever looked good in my 90-bottle wine refrigerator, then binge-watching a show I'd seen a hundred times before. It was a temporary escape and a way to dull the pain of feeling out of place in a career I worked decades to create. I knew it was a poor way to cope with my feelings of inadequacy and imposter syndrome, not to mention it was detrimental to my overall health. I slept horribly and woke up each morning feeling run down and irritable. On the last day of January 2023, divine intervention showed up in the form of a friend celebrating 100 days alcohol-free on social media, sharing how it had changed her life. I knew I needed to make a change, so I committed to do the same thing. I was terrified I wouldn't be able to do it, so I told very few people.

For years, I lived out of alignment and in a funk with alcohol, but once I eliminated it from my life, I began acknowledging my emotions and working through them. To say my life began to change dramatically would be an understatement. I was sleeping better, waking up with more energy, and showing up in my daily life as a better version of myself. I was figuring out how to navigate a life without using alcohol as a crutch to "unwind" and escape the emotional baggage of imposter syndrome and misalignment in my role.

Fast-forward to Day 40 of being alcohol-free when that pivotal, scary conversation with my boss happened about how my role was evolving and how I wasn't the best person for it. Deep down, I *knew* I was in the wrong "lane." But I was scared about what it would say about me if I wasn't successful in the role as it evolved. I was telling myself all kinds of stories about being unsuccessful, a failure, "not enough" and that I was letting the other women in the company down. When I uttered that terrifying statement to my boss, I was putting it all on the line. But I had a deep knowing in my gut that it was my truth.

What followed was an open dialogue about re-focusing my responsibilities to align with my areas of strength. The business development responsibilities could go to another person on the team and they'd backfill with someone with more experience in the nonprofit sector. I could operate in my areas of strength and continue to add value to a company I loved working for. As a bonus, this change opened up more bandwidth for me to focus on building my coaching business, which I had started years before.

I can confidently say that navigating those few months of tough conversations and recasting my career would have been infinitely more difficult had I continued drinking alcohol. I was getting out of the funk I was in by making decisions that were in alignment with my values, skill sets, and passion.

Living in Alignment

I realize that this phrase may not resonate with everyone, so let me explain. "Living in alignment," or living "congruently," isn't just a buzzword or a fleeting trend—it's a profound shift in how we approach life, particularly when it comes to our purpose, mindset, and health. It's about consciously aligning our actions, decisions, and values with our true selves. Picture it as a state of flow and harmony, where the choices we make resonate deeply with who we are at our core. For me, it's been a journey of self-discovery, of peeling back the layers of expectations, societal norms, and false stories I've believed to uncover what truly matters to me. It's about honoring my experience, leveraging my unique skills, and staying true to my values, even when it's not easy.

Living in alignment isn't about perfection—it's about self-awareness, authenticity, and growth. It's about saying yes to the things that light us up and confidently saying no to anything that doesn't serve us. It's a journey I've embarked on, and one that has brought me a newfound sense of freedom and purpose. And it's one I'm passionate about sharing because I believe that when we live in alignment with our true selves, we unlock our untapped potential and create a ripple effect of positive change in our lives and the lives of those around us. Sounds amazing, doesn't it? If it sounds unattainable, I want you to stay with me here. When you decide to get out of the funk you are in, you've actually taken the first step. And with each step comes more momentum in the pursuit. You don't have to have done all the work to feel the freedom and fulfillment that comes with living congruently. The feeling comes with each decision you make along the way.

Getting Out of the Funk in Your Purpose

As I shared in my story earlier, I was committed to "climbing the corporate ladder" for the better part of the last 15 years. I believed that responsibility, title, salary, and influence equaled success. This pursuit fueled my sense of self-worth and confidence. However, this misaligned mentality eventually landed me in a role where 50% of my responsibilities were wildly outside of my background and skills. If you find yourself mentally and emotionally drained at the end of the day, feeling stuck or stagnant, itching to do something else, and dreading the next morning, you are most definitely in a funk. The good news is that you don't have to stay there!

If you are in a funk with your purpose or career, the next best step is to ask yourself the following questions:

- What activities or tasks make me lose track of time and feel most energized?
- What strengths, talents, and skills do I possess that can be utilized in meaningful ways?
- What impact do I aspire to make in my community or the world?
- When do I feel most alive and aligned with my true self?
- What problems or challenges do I feel most compelled to solve?

These questions will help uncover the activities and interests that resonate with your purpose. Ideally, your purpose aligns with your career, but it doesn't have to. Understanding what truly drives you can guide you toward finding fulfillment both in and outside of your professional life. Whether your purpose is directly tied to your job or pursued through hobbies, a side hustle, or volunteering, recognizing it is the first step toward living a more aligned and meaningful life.

When I gained alignment in my corporate work, I discovered a new sense of freedom and empowerment. It felt like I was finally in the correct "lane" on the company's six-lane highway. The mental and emotional weight of feeling like an imposter lifted which unlocked a new level of creativity, engagement, and energy.

If you're in a funk with your purpose, remember that you don't have to stay there. By identifying what truly energizes you and taking steps toward integrating an outlet for it into your life, you will experience more joy and fulfillment.

Getting Out of the Funk in Your Mindset

Have you had a barrage of negative thoughts or limiting beliefs and can't snap out of it? Being in this place can take us down the proverbial rabbit hole where we see each of life's circumstances as happening *to us*, rather than *for us*. I've been in a mindset funk like this more times than I can count, but I've learned how to pivot when I'm there and unlock an incredibly powerful and positive outlook on life.

When I'm in a mindset funk, the first thing I do is ask myself a series of questions to assess what I've been consuming in my "whitespace" or free time. This practice has been so effective that I've formalized it into a tool called the Mindset Inventory™. At its core, the Mindset Inventory™ is based on this foundational principle:

What we consume on a regular basis shapes our thoughts, our thoughts mold our beliefs, our beliefs fuel our actions, and our actions dictate our results. If we want different results in life, we need to go back to what we are consuming and pivot.

Without realizing it, we can reinforce negative thoughts and limiting beliefs by consuming content that focuses too much on problems and conflicts. Social media can also trap us in a cycle of comparison. Constantly seeing others' "curated highlights" can make us feel inadequate, envious, and full of self-doubt—all fueling a mindset funk. So ask yourself:

- How often do you visit websites that inspire or motivate you?
- How often do you read or listen to books that help you grow personally or professionally?
- How much time do you spend scrolling social media or watching YouTube?
- How much time do you spend playing video games or games on your phone?
- How often do you binge-watch TV shows or movies?
- How often do you feel your "whitespace" time is used productively?
- How often do you spend time with people who make you feel positive and uplifted?
- How often do you follow an established morning routine?

Once we have an awareness of what is fueling our mindset, we can make small changes to pivot. In all my years of coaching, what I've found is that people generally make big sweeping changes when they are highly motivated. However, motivation is fleeting. Life happens, and we revert to what we are most familiar with, whether or not it serves us. Our brains are wired to keep us in safe, familiar territory, but ultimately, stuck if we seek to grow and make an impact.

The people who win long-term make small changes consistently over time. Here are some things I've done to shift what I was consuming that helped establish a more positive mindset:

- Curating my social media feeds by unfollowing negative people and groups, and following those who inspire, encourage, and motivate me.
- Subscribing to and listening to podcasts that uplift and inspire me.
- Limiting time with people who are overly negative or stuck in a victim mindset.
- Temporarily or permanently removing games and streaming apps from my phone

Being stuck in a mindset funk doesn't have to be permanent. By using the Mindset Inventory and making small, consistent changes to what we consume, we can begin to consume content that helps create a more positive, optimistic outlook.

Getting Out of the Funk in Your Health

Ever felt uncomfortable in your own skin? Have you found yourself stuck in a cycle of unhealthy eating and drinking habits, with your doctor constantly urging you to make lifestyle changes to avoid medications? If so, you might be in a funk with your health. Trust me, I've been there, and it's definitely not a place you want to camp out. Five years ago, I hit my breaking point: the discomfort of staying the same outweighed the fear of change. I was obese, constantly exhausted, drinking a lot, sedentary, and relying on medication because my innards needed pharmaceutical intervention to stave off serious medical conditions.

Especially when it comes to our physical well-being, sometimes it takes hitting rock bottom to realize that something's gotta give. We know deep down that we're in a funk, but taking that first step toward change can feel daunting. But trust me, it's worth it. The increased confidence and freedom that accompanies gaining alignment in our physical health is life-changing.

Over the last 5 years, I've been focused on improving my health by saying goodbye to obesity and alcohol and hello to exercise, fueling my body well and with functional medicine. I didn't tackle these all at the same time, but through the process, I've learned a couple of game-changing things.

Don't Go It Alone

Making changes to your physical health is always easier when you have support. When things get tough (and it will), it's tempting to go it alone, but that's actually when we need others the most. Surrounding ourselves with people who are either walking the same path or have already been through it, is pivotal. When I shed 50 pounds back in 2019, I relied on a simple nutrition plan, along with the guidance of a health coach and a supportive community. And when I decided to take a break from alcohol, I found inspiration from people on social media who are living an alcohol-free life. Being part of a community of people with similar goals and experiences not only lifts you up but also fuels your determination to keep going.

Making a Decision Creates Momentum

The moment you make a decision, momentum begins to build. I used to (incorrectly) believe that achieving the goal, crossing the finish line, or reaching a desired number on the scale would create momentum. It isn't the end goal being achieved, but the act of deciding to begin, coupled with taking an aligned action, that sparks the energy and sense of possibility for a better future.

After the initial call with a functional medicine practitioner regarding my autoimmune thyroid disease, I felt a renewed sense of hope and possibility. The energy and optimism I felt following our call confirmed that I was on the right path. Although it took a few months of following a tailored protocol to notice significant improvements, simply deciding to pursue the functional medicine route and scheduling the first call dramatically shifted my outlook. The key lesson? Momentum begins the moment you make a decision and take the next best step toward making it happen.

It's a Journey, We Don't Ever Arrive

Pursuing alignment in our physical health is like laundry… it's never done. I share this not to discourage you, but rather to encourage you. When you prioritize your health, you're not just taking care of your body—you're also creating space to fully embrace your purpose and find deeper fulfillment in life.

As we age, we will inevitably face various health challenges that offer us new opportunities for growth. Each challenge presents a chance to make a decision, take action, and connect with a community of individuals who understand and can support us along the way.

Deciding to get out of the funk is the first step toward living in alignment. The moment you choose to make a change, you're already on your way. Each step you take builds momentum. You don't need to have it all figured out to start feeling the empowerment of living congruently. That feeling grows with every decision you make. So, let's embrace this venture together, knowing that each step brings us closer to living a more fulfilled life.

This chapter is a preview of Molly's upcoming solo book What the Funk?! A Practical Guide to Getting Out of the Funk You Are in with Your Health, Mindset & Purpose *which will be published in January 2025. To connect with Molly, visit www.nextbeststep.co.*

Martha Smith

Martie M Smith. Com LLC
International Award Winning Author

http://linkedin.com/in/martie-smith-8b062025
https://www.facebook.com/MarthaSmith07
https://www.instagram.com/vinnersary
https://martiemsmith.com/

Martie Smith, an internationally recognized poet laureate and author, shares inspiring tales of resilience worldwide. Through collaborations on works like "Grateful Hearts" and "Ripples of Grace," she uplifts others with her stories. Despite facing surgeries and emotional challenges, her unwavering faith in God and the support of her husband shine through. She has been a personal trainer in North Carolina, promoting mind, body, and soul well-being. While not having children of her own, she has positively impacted countless youths over three decades with her wisdom and faith. Taking her message to the global stage, Martie's speaking focuses on perseverance and hope, aiming to inspire audiences of all ages. Her journey is a testament to resilience and the power of a positive outlook in life.

The Journey of Resilience

By Martha Smith

The Essence of Resilience

In life's journey of self-discovery, resilience often serves as the flickering light that guides us through the darkest moments. It is not just about enduring difficult times; it's about rising, each time stronger, with newfound courage and determination to move forward despite the seemingly insurmountable obstacles. Resilience is the quiet yet powerful force that pushes us to overcome adversity, transforming each setback into a stepping stone. For many women, resilience is not merely a trait or an occasional burst of strength but an intrinsic way of life—a constant companion that shapes who we are and how we navigate the world.

My resilience journey began at a tender age, filled with innocence, hope, and wonder. I was just seven years old when I first encountered whispers of the adversity that would forge the foundations of my strength. I was told I was not planned. A mistake that planted a seed of perseverance that I would amount to something one day. At the same time, my family had relocated, and moving to a new school in an unfamiliar city felt like an overwhelming challenge. The unfamiliarity of the situation was isolating; I felt lost and alone, surrounded by faces I didn't know.

Reflecting on this early experience, I recognize that resilience isn't solely about facing hardship; it's about how we choose to respond to adversity, whether small or large. And the truth is, no one's journey is isolated. The stories of resilience are woven into

The larger tapestry of women's collective experience. Each thread represents a unique journey, yet all are part of a shared narrative of strength, hope, and transformation. Collectively, these stories serve as a testament to the indomitable spirit of women—a reminder that no matter the challenges we face, we have the power to rise above them, emerging stronger and more resilient on the other side.

Foundations of Strength

Childhood is often a time of innocence, wonder, and discovery. However, for many, it can also be when we first encounter challenges that test the boundaries of our strength and shape our future resilience. As a young child, my first real encounter with hardship came when I moved to the new school. I was naive, and the unfamiliar environment felt overwhelming. The faces of strangers and the uncertainty weighed heavily on me. But in this discomfort, I found something invaluable: the kindness of others.

Through this experience, I learned that resilience is not about enduring hardship alone; it's about the power of connection. The smiles and friendship extended to me by my classmates helped to ease some of my fears, offering me a lifeline that gave me the courage to reach out and forge new bonds. In those moments, I learned the value of empathy, openness, and the importance of support systems—lessons that would carry me through life.

These early experiences taught me resilience is not simply about enduring or persevering in isolation. It is about recognizing that strength is found in vulnerability and that the willingness to open ourselves up to others can be a powerful act of resilience. These lessons of empathy and openness became the foundation of my resilience, allowing me to navigate future challenges in adolescence and adulthood with the understanding that I didn't have to go through anything alone.

Navigating Turbulent Waters

Adolescence often presents a whirlwind of emotional turmoil and self-doubt, and for me, it was no different. A storm of confusion marked the teenage years—academic expectations, social pressures, and personal identity clashed in a struggle for balance. It was a time when I questioned who I was, what I stood for, and how I fit into the world. There were moments of overwhelming self-doubt, exacerbated by external pressures to conform, succeed, and fit in. The turbulence of those years often made it feel like I was caught in a storm, without an anchor to steady myself.

Amid this chaos, I found my refuge in creativity. I turned to art and self-expression to process the inner complexity of my emotions. Art became my anchor, a safe space to explore my inner world without fear of judgment. Through creative pursuits, I learned that resilience wasn't just about enduring hardship but finding a healthy outlet for emotions, a way to express and channel the storm inside. These creative endeavors didn't just soothe my soul;

They allowed me to discover new depths of strength and self-awareness. I realized that resilience is not about suppressing feelings or putting on a brave face; it's about finding ways to express and process our vulnerabilities to help us grow.

The creative process taught me resilience is more than just surviving turbulent times—it's about thriving within them. It's about discovering what keeps us grounded when everything else feels uncertain. Whether it's art, music, writing, or any other passion, these outlets help us weather the storms of life, offering us a path to self-discovery and strength.

Independence and Responsibility

The transition into adulthood is marked by a desire for independence, accompanied by the weight of new responsibilities. At nineteen, I stood on the precipice of adulthood, filled with excitement and trepidation. This was a time of newfound freedom, but it also came with the realization that I was responsible for my life. The decisions I made from this point on would shape my future, and the weight of these expectations often felt overwhelming.

During these early years of adulthood, I learned resilience on a whole new level. Every setback and every disappointment tested my resolve, yet each also helped me grow stronger. I began to understand that resilience is not a destination but

A journey—a continuous process of picking ourselves up, learning from our experiences, and moving forward with a renewed sense of purpose. Each hurdle I encountered tempered my spirit, teaching me the value of perseverance.

I realized that resilience is about more than just bouncing back from failure; it's about learning to embrace challenges as opportunities for growth. It's about recognizing that every obstacle we face is an opportunity to learn, adapt, and transform. The early lessons I learned about responsibility, perseverance, and self-reliance would continue to serve me well as I navigated the complexities of adult life.

Embracing Change and Growth

By reaching my mid-thirties, I found myself at a crossroads in my career. My chosen path no longer fulfilled me, and I began questioning the direction of my professional life. This period of reflection and reevaluation was daunting. I had invested so much time and energy into a career that no longer aligned with my passions or values, and the thought of changing course felt overwhelming. Yet, during this time, I also discovered the transformative power of resilience.

With courage and determination, I decided to take a leap of faith and pursue a new direction more aligned with my true self. Leaving the familiar behind was difficult, and the transition into a new field was uncertain. There were moments when I doubted my ability to succeed, but each challenge I faced became worth pursuing.

It was a lesson in resilience. I learned to embrace the discomfort of change, seeing it as a necessary catalyst for growth and self-discovery.

I realized that resilience isn't just about enduring hardship—it's about embracing change and seeing it as an opportunity for growth. It's about having the courage to step outside our comfort zones, pursue our passions, and trust in our ability to adapt and thrive, even when the path ahead is uncertain.

The Balancing Act of Life

As I entered middle age, life became a delicate balancing act. The demands of career, family, and personal fulfillment often felt like they were pulling me in different directions, threatening to overwhelm my sense of equilibrium. Yet, through the years, I had learned the importance of resilience—not as a means to avoid difficulty but as a way to adapt to it.

Experience has taught me that resilience is not about trying to control every aspect of life but about learning to flow with the changes that come our way. Life's challenges, I discovered, are not obstacles to be feared but opportunities for growth and transformation. By accepting this truth, I courageously embraced life's uncertainties with grace.

The key to maintaining resilience during this period was balance. I learned the importance of self-care, of making time for the things that brought me joy and fulfillment. I also learned the power of setting boundaries—of saying no to the things.

That did not align with my values or contribute to my growth. This was not always easy, but it was necessary. I found resilience is not just about surviving life's challenges; it's about thriving within them by prioritizing our well-being and honoring our needs.

The Shared Experience of Women

Throughout my journey, I understood that resilience is an individual endeavor and a collective experience that binds us together as women. While our journeys are unique, common threads of strength, courage, and determination unite us. We each face our personal, professional, or societal battles, and when these challenges arise, we draw strength from one another. The solidarity in our struggles creates a powerful bond—a sense of sisterhood that transcends differences and unites us in our quest for growth and transformation.

True resilience is not about suppressing our emotions or pretending everything is fine. It's about embracing our vulnerabilities, acknowledging our fears, and finding the courage to overcome them. We are not defined by our challenges but by how we respond to them—grace, strength, and determination. Recognizing this is an act of self-love and self-empowerment. It declares that we are worthy of joy, fulfillment, and purpose.

By embracing our resilience and sharing our stories, we create a space where others can see themselves reflected and feel validated in their own experiences. We remind each other that we are not alone in our struggles, have the power to overcome adversity, and can emerge more robust and more resilient than ever before. This shared experience of resilience is a powerful force—a ripple effect of hope and empowerment that extends far beyond our journeys.

Inspiring Others

The power of sharing our stories of resilience cannot be overstated. In sharing our experiences, we foster connection, understanding, and empathy. Resilience is not a one-size-fits-all concept; it manifests in diverse ways, reflecting the rich tapestry of human experience. From the young girl who finds the courage to speak out against injustice to the single mother who works tirelessly to provide for her children to the older woman who faces the challenges of aging with grace and dignity—each of these stories is a testament to strength, courage, and resilience that God grants.

By sharing our stories, we create a space where others can see themselves in our experiences. We inspire, we uplift, and we empower each other. In doing so, we create that ripple effect—a wave of hope, strength, and resilience that reaches far beyond our individual lives and touches the lives of many others.

Embracing the Journey of Resilience

Looking back on my journey, I am filled with pride and accomplishment. I faced countless challenges and obstacles, each shaping me into the woman I am today. I embraced my vulnerabilities, found strength in struggles, and rose above adversity with grace and determination. Through these experiences, I have discovered the true power of resilience: the ability to transform, grow, and thrive in the face of life's most significant challenges.

As I move forward into the next chapter of my life, I do so with a heart filled with gratitude and a spirit imbued with resilience. I am ready to face whatever challenges and adventures await me on the next leg of my remarkable journey. The path ahead will not always be easy, but I can navigate it gracefully and with courage and faith. I know that no matter the challenges that come my way, I will rise above them, guided by an unwavering sense of strength and resilience.

Resilience is not about reaching a final destination but embracing growth and transformation at every step. It is about finding the courage to face and overcome our fears, knowing that we are not defined by our circumstances but by how we respond. It is about realizing that we are capable of far more than we ever imagined and understanding that we can shape our destinies.

As I continue this journey, I am reminded of the strength and courage within each of us. I am inspired by the stories of resilience shared with me, and I am grateful for the wisdom and strength these stories have imparted. Each story is a thread in the larger tapestry of our collective experience, woven together to create a powerful narrative of resilience, hope, and transformation in life.

I am thankful for every challenge that has tested my resolve and for every triumph that has affirmed my strength. I am grateful for the women who have shared their stories with me, showing me that resilience is not a solitary pursuit but a shared journey that binds us together in our quest for growth and transformation. As I look toward the future, I am filled with hope and excitement for what lies ahead.

Resilience as a Lifelong Journey

The journey of resilience is a lifelong one—a continuous cycle of growth, adaptation, and renewal. It is not a straight path but a winding road with twists, turns, peaks, and valleys. Challenges test our strength and shape our character, offering valuable lessons that help us navigate adversity.

Resilience is not something we are born with but something we develop over time through experiences and choices. It is a skill cultivated through practice and reflection, strengthened by embracing our vulnerabilities and facing our fears. By adopting this mindset, we see challenges not as obstacles to avoid but as opportunities for growth.

My journey taught me that resilience is not about being invincible or never experiencing pain or hardship. It is about acknowledging our struggles and finding the strength to rise above them. It is about embracing our imperfections and learning to love ourselves, even when we feel broken or lost. It is about trusting in our ability to heal and grow, even when the path ahead is unclear.

Empowering the Next Generation

Reflecting on my journey, I am reminded of the importance of empowering the next generation of women to embrace resilience. We are responsible for sharing our stories, mentoring and guiding, supporting, and uplifting those who come after us. In doing so, we create a legacy of strength and empowerment that transcends generations.

We must teach the next generation that resilience is not about being perfect or having all the answers. It is about being authentic, embracing our vulnerabilities, and finding the courage to face our fears. We must encourage them to pursue their passions, take risks, and embrace change as an opportunity for growth. Most importantly, we must show them that they are not alone in their struggles and that they have the power to overcome whatever challenges come their way.

By empowering the next generation, we create a powerful narrative of resilience that inspires and uplifts others. We show young women that they are capable of far more than they ever imagined and that they have the strength and courage to shape their

Destinies. We remind them that resilience is not just a quality to possess but a journey to embrace—a continuous process of growth and transformation that unfolds throughout our lives.

Celebrating Resilience in All Its Forms

As I close this chapter of my journey, I am grateful for the resilience that has shaped my life—the lessons learned, the challenges overcome, and the strength I have gained. I am thankful for the women who have shared their stories with me and inspired me to keep moving forward, no matter the obstacles I face. I am grateful to God for allowing me to see beyond the pain and adversity.

Resilience looks different for everyone, and there is no right or wrong way to be resilient. For some, resilience means raising their voice and advocating for themselves. For others, it means leaving a toxic situation and starting anew. Yet, for others, it may mean simply finding the strength to keep going, even when everything is falling apart.

Whatever form resilience takes, it is worthy of celebration. It is a testament to our strength and courage, a reminder that we can overcome challenges and inspire others. Resilience is a powerful force for positive change and transformation in our lives and those around us. Let's strengthen our resilience, evolve with adversity, and grow.

The Power of Resilience

Resilience is not a destination but a journey. It is a continuous process of growth and transformation that unfolds throughout our lives. It is about finding the strength to rise above adversity, the courage to embrace change, and the wisdom to learn from our experiences. Resilience is recognizing that we are not defined by our circumstances but by how we respond to them.

As we continue this journey, remember that we are not alone. We are part of a larger tapestry of strength and courage, woven together by the stories of countless women who have faced challenges and emerged stronger. Let us draw strength from one another, knowing that we are all capable of far more than we ever imagined.

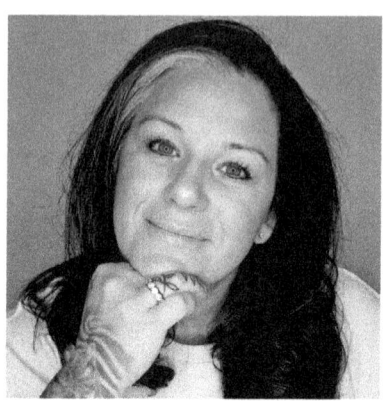

KB Vega

InspiHER Empire
Inspirationalist & Chief Empowerment Officer

https://www.linkedin.com/in/karla-boccabella-vega-01b933235/
https://www.facebook.com/inspiherempire
https://www.instagram.com/inspiherempire
https://inspiherempire.com/

Say hello to KB Vega, a proud Bostonian with strong ties to Massachusetts. As the Chief Empowerment Officer of InspiHER Empire, KB puts her heart and soul into her clothing and lifestyle brand that serves as a beacon of empowerment for women everywhere. By promoting self-love, body positivity, and confidence, KB's work motivates women to celebrate their uniqueness and strive for greatness. Despite her current success, KB acknowledges that her journey wasn't without challenges. In her younger years, she grappled with self-doubt, body image issues, and confidence struggles, which have all contributed to shaping her into the fierce advocate for empowerment she is today. With dedication and a firm belief in the power of self-acceptance, KB continues to uplift and inspire women to break free from societal norms and embrace their inner strength.

More Than Enough

By KB Vega

Finding My Worth in a World of Disappointment

"It's a Karla, not a Carlo." That one sentence flipped the script of my life forever. A girl, not a boy. Another addition to our clan of daughters. I could picture it vividly. My mom, a whirlwind of emotions—happy, excited, and nervous all at once—stepping into motherhood for the third time, years after her last daughter was born. My conception was a surprise, catching both my parents off guard. And it didn't change when the time came for me to enter this world. Mom reveled in the unexpected joy, but for Dad, it was a different story. Let's just say his reaction wasn't exactly a standing ovation. Mom spilled the tea years later: Dad wasn't exactly thrilled about expanding the team roster, especially not with another girl. He was disappointed and he had his heart set on a son to carry on the family legacy ever since my Mom became pregnant the first time. Understandable, but as a newborn, absorbing all this was a tad overwhelming. Little did I know, that seemingly harmless remark would echo through the years, shaping my journey of self-discovery and worth.

Growing up, my family dynamic was quite the spectacle. Picture this: My dad, the ultimate hustler, juggling multiple restaurants and businesses simultaneously. You can already guess how that colored my childhood. Dad was hardly ever home, buried under the weight of his work commitments. Left to fend for herself, Mom would drag me along to Dad's restaurant, promising a cozy family dinner. But reality rarely matched the picture-perfect scenario. Instead of quality time with Dad, I found myself vying for attention amidst a sea of customers and employees who seemed to hold a higher rank on Dad's priority list. It was as if we were extras in his life, always waiting for our turn in the spotlight. Those moments left a bitter taste, reinforcing the belief that I wasn't quite good enough, never quite important. And that feeling? It stuck with me like gum on a shoe.

As I matured and time rolled on, the relationship with my dad became a roller coaster, filled with highs and lows. But amidst it all, that single comment lingered like a persistent storm cloud, casting a shadow over my thoughts for years to come. I constantly found myself striving to earn approval not only from him but from others, desperate to prove my worth and secure their affection. It's a lousy sensation, let me tell you, when your own value feels like it's constantly up for debate.

Around that time, my parents decided to split up, a pretty unusual move back then. I was just eleven, too young to fully understand the storm that was brewing in our family. All I knew was that things were changing rapidly and not for the better. There was a phase when my older sisters cut off contact with Dad, but I stuck by him. It felt like I was the only one he paid attention to during those days. Maybe it was because I was the only one who didn't shut him out, despite whatever he did to tear our family apart—a lot of which I was too young to understand. Who knows what his real reasons were? All I knew was that for a while, I felt like I mattered most to him. But, as life would have it, that didn't last long.

When I entered high school, a lot of things that were kept from me when I was younger about Dad's doings, were shed to light and I started to see what really went down. I found out things that I never knew before. Like that, my Dad told my Mom right after I was born, that he was no longer in love with her. He was engaging in adulterous activities and my Mom thought that having a baby would keep him at home. So, I was a plot twist, unplanned, and a ploy to get my dad to stay? Was that the original plan? Maybe this is why I am such a spitfire. So people know that I am here and I am here to stay! Back then, especially finding these things out though, I didn't think that way.

I started to blame myself for their divorce. If only I wasn't born, they would have been together still. If only I was the right gender, maybe things would have been different. It fucked me up completely and slowly but surely, these thoughts took a toll on me and my self-worth. This feeling was constant, leading me down a path of self-mutilation, eating disorders, drugs and even attempting suicide because I felt like I just wasn't good enough and not worthy to be on this earth. By then, my self-esteem had plummeted to rock bottom, and the constant battle to justify my worth to others was draining beyond measure. It was undoubtedly one of the darkest periods of my life, plunging me into the depths of severe depression. The struggle became so overwhelming that medication seemed like the only option. However, it merely masked the surface wounds, failing to address the deeper issues rooted in my childhood experiences.

Having these thoughts about myself and finding out the truth about my parents' tumultuous relationship, I became very promiscuous because I just didn't give a shit anymore. I found myself in toxic relationships, trusting people who only used me, and I didn't give a damn about taking care of myself. My whole perception of myself was completely lost. I was depressed, I was struggling with my self-image, my body was changing (I actually got pregnant twice and in both times I was forced to have abortions by my mother), and my family life was non-existent. So, I tuned it all out with who and what was giving me attention and it just happened to be with older teenage boys. Fun fact that I should have known back then: horny teenage boys prey on the weak and don't give a shit what you are going through. They know all the right things to say and all the right things to do to get what they want. And that's exactly what happened. Which then, in turn, deepened my self-hatred even more.

I used to sabotage myself constantly in pursuit of fitting in. Back in high school, I convinced myself that if I changed myself enough, I could finally belong. If I could just be thin, maybe then the popular girls would accept me. If I acted promiscuous, maybe the boys would finally pay attention. And if I excelled in school, maybe my parents would be proud. If I self-mutilated, then the hurt that I felt would go away. Because that makes sense, right? I was already hurting, so adding more hurt would make me feel better. That was what I thought back then. It makes me sad to think that I went to such extremes to be accepting of myself and accepting to others.

Even partaking in sports like the cheerleading team, seemed like a path to acceptance, because, let's face it, cheerleading is definitely a sport, no debate there. But back then, it wasn't thought of as a sport like football or softball, and once again, I found myself yearning to be a part of something. After a terrible car accident caused by black ice in my senior year in high school, I realized I needed to make some big changes. But even though the crash shook me, my feelings of worthlessness overshadowed the trauma. I couldn't shake the guilt of blaming myself for the accident, convinced it happened because I was rushing to cheerleading practice.

These thoughts haunted me throughout high school and followed me into college, where they morphed into a cycle of partying, substance abuse, and even cosmetic surgery to boost my confidence. But it didn't end there. Even after college, I found myself in a toxic relationship with an abusive, alcoholic partner. When I became pregnant, I felt like a failure when complications led to a loss. The weight of depression crushed me as I grappled with feelings of inadequacy.

Fleeing to NYC seemed like a fresh start, but it only led me deeper into a destructive pattern of drug addiction. I was desperate to prove that I could be the life of the party, even if it meant sacrificing my own well-being. Until one day, a terrifying experience with drugs forced me to confront my worthiness. I realized I deserved better. I left behind the drugs and returned to Massachusetts, where I supported my partner in building his business and worked a steady job at the local hospital for eight years. I was actually living a boring but normal life.

Slowly but surely, my perception of myself began to shift. I stopped letting the voices from my past dictate my worth. Instead, I started to appreciate myself for who I truly was. This transformation empowered me to become the strong person I am today and to start my own clothing business by helping and inspiring women to feel good about themselves, especially through the struggles of adversity.

I also learned that self-respect is the foundation for demanding respect from others. There's a saying that goes, "Treat yourself well so others know how to treat you." Despite the challenges and disappointments I've faced, I've learned to never let anyone diminish my worth again. I am more than enough, have always been more than enough and I refuse to settle for anything less. And my name is fucking KARLA, not Carlo!

Jadira Amaya

Business Growth Strategist & Mindset Coach

https://www.facebook.com/staywildwithyadi
https://www.instagram.com/staywildwithyadi
http://www.staywildwithyadi.com/

Jadira Amaya, known as "Yadi," is an entrepreneur, author, business growth strategist, and mindset coach dedicated to empowering others to live authentically. Her journey from teen mom and cancer survivor to successful entrepreneur is a testament to her resilience. Having broken the cycle of abuse, Jadira's vulnerability and strength inspire others to embrace their story and overcome adversity. Passionate about helping women shift their mindset and recognize their worth, Jadira guides them to unlock their fullest potential. Through her writing, new podcast, and transformative "I'm a Badass" list and course, she provides tools for women to step into their power, live authentically, and create the lives they desire.

A ROSE AMIDST THE THORNS

By Jadira Amaya

Uncovering Beauty and Strength in Adversity

I often reflect on the path that led me here, one marked by trials and triumphs, by heartache and healing. The journey wasn't easy, but it shaped me into the <u>resilient</u> woman I am today. My story is full of tenacity, perseverance, and empowerment, just like a rose. This is my narrative, one that I hope will inspire and remind you to always admire and embrace beauty, despite the thorns encountered along the way.

My childhood was tainted by turbulent instability and domestic violence which permanently cast dark shadows over our home. My parents divorced when I was 6 years old, which only intensified the sense of uncertainty as we moved from place to place, including 3 years living in El Grullo, Mexico, during my 4–6th grade school years. I was a victim of sexual abuse as early as 6 or 7 lasting until my early teens. The safe, nurturing environment every child deserves was unknown to me. I was the eldest of three siblings, and although my brothers and I never went without the necessities to survive, I lacked stability, parental guidance, and affection, which created an overwhelming sense of longing and unworthiness. This void was only deepened by the trauma of sexual abuse, which left me feeling isolated and abandoned, alone in a world where I starved for affection, love, and connection. Instead, I learned to navigate life filled with fear and uncertainty. I was vulnerable and quiet, which made me an easy target for the predators that lurked in the shadows.

By my early teens the angst and isolation became unbearable; desperate to escape the scxual abuse and neglect from home, I ran away, seeking solace in the streets. By that time, the sexual abuse had escalated to rape, with no parental guidance or shielding, and desperate for the need to belong, I began skipping school and getting into trouble. The allure of gang life, promiscuity, and the thrill of rebellion seemed like the only way to gain the attention and love I desperately needed from my mother. I ran away from home countless times, each time lasting longer than the previous; I would eventually be returned unwillingly in handcuffs or by a court order. Ultimately, my mother didn't want me back at home, I remember her telling law enforcement to "lock her up" or "take her away, I just don't want her here!"

The irony of the trauma which cut scars so deep that I was consumed by the thought of taking my own life was my will and determination to survive for I knew that I not only must persevere for myself, but I was now 15 years old and pregnant.

Several pivotal moments encapsulated my journey toward change. The first one was the birth of my only daughter, Jasmine. I was in my first semester of high school when I found out I was pregnant. Prior to this discovery, I was barely attending school, smoking weed, underage drinking, having unprotected sex, and stealing car stereos in the school parking lot with my boyfriend, the soon-to-be father of my child. Regardless that I was only 15 and did not have a learner's permit, he taught me how to drive. He was a junior in high school and drove an old rustic brown Cutlass Oldsmobile lowrider. Although his English was fragmented from having migrated from Veracruz, Mexico, just two years prior, he was a schoolboy. He was smart and thoroughly enjoyed his studies; in fact, it was I who convinced him to ditch school, which ultimately led to my daughter being conceived in the back of his lowrider. When I told my mother that I was expecting, I was given an ultimatum, either abort my pregnancy or leave the house permanently; without hesitation, I chose the latter. I moved in with my boyfriend, where we resided with his older sister, husband, and two kids in a small one-bedroom apartment and slept on their living room pull-out mattress. We both dropped out of school and began selling drugs and hustling to get a place of our own. I instantly became an "adult" overnight; my daughter was on her way and unbeknownst to me she was everything I never knew I always wanted or needed to change my path's trajectory.

My second profound moment came with another harsh reality; I was 8 months pregnant when I became privy to the fact that detectives were searching for me in connection with the kidnapping and murder of a local woman. I remember pleading to the officers, "Look at me, I am ready to have a baby at any moment!" They proceeded to tell me that the culmination of my juvenile record, gang affiliation, and witness descriptions matched my profile perfectly. At that time, I was not only affiliated with a gang, but my boyfriend was the leader of our gang, the Brown Pride Tokers. Yes, we were dealing crack cocaine and marijuana, among other minor felonies… but kidnapping and murder?! Absolutely not! That situation and other frequent encounters with the law intensified the need for a drastic change, but that didn't come until it was mandated by the juvenile judicial system and child protective services. I was 16 when a narcotic team raided our home, yelling at us to get down on the ground with our hands behind our backs. My boyfriend was taken into custody; because I was a minor, they called my mother. There I went, back to the original place of my suffering, yet this time, I was accompanied by my infant daughter.

Upon my boyfriend's release from the correctional facility, our relationship deteriorated. His anger projected onto me, and I ultimately became on the receiving end of his clenched fists. I left and at age 19 I became a single mother to a three-year-old child. He was murdered two years later.

Too young to be "the perfect mom" yet I solely bore the responsibility of being two parents in one. The 19-year-old girl in me took two steps backward. I indulged in sex with multiple partners, re-affiliated with gang life, and either brought my daughter with me regardless of the risk or consequence, or depended on a friend who accepted alcohol and cigarettes in lieu of cash to take care of her.

The day that my boyfriend succumbed from his gunshot wound was the day I said my final goodbye to the gang life. I wanted more for my daughter and me. As serendipitous as it sounds, I began working full-time for the State at a juvenile correctional facility where I vowed to never look back.

Perhaps the most significant moment of my life coupled with the yearning to share my story, was my battle against breast cancer in 2011. The diagnosis felt like a thousand pricks from the sharpest thorns; a moment where time stood still and cancer seized my mind. There was an overwhelming sense of fear and uncertainty, not just about my future but my life. I contemplated whether this may be karma or the burden for all of my sins. There I was, 31, a survivor of a tumultuous childhood and young adulthood, only to once again fight from becoming a victim of a life-threatening ailment. The journey through this battle was one that pushed me to the very edges of my physical and emotional well-being. There were moments when I felt like giving up when the pain and weight of it all seemed too much to bear. After the final treatment and surgery, the oncologist confirmed that the cancer was in remission, it was a defining moment of relief and profound transformation. Surviving cancer wasn't just a physical triumph; it was a testament to the strength of the human spirit, the power of hope, and the unbreakable will to live.

Shall we speak about love? It was 2007 when I had that one significant moment where my garden came into full bloom. A kiss from another woman enriched my soil so plentiful that I knew my flowers would never be the same. It may have taken another 15 years of cultivating this garden before I came upon one different seed, my sunflower, of whom I will speak more later in this memoir.

While I skipped most of middle school and dropped out of high school during my freshman year having only earned a 0.5 credit, I was determined to succeed. I enrolled in community college a few times but dropped out when I felt overwhelmed. Despite having only an eighth-grade education, I understood that knowledge was a powerful tool that could help me break free from the cycle of poverty and adversity. I immersed myself in books, podcasts, sought out mentors, and absorbed everything I could about business and personal development. In 2016, I created and launched my personal clothing brand, Wildjay, and opened my very own storefront downtown.

One of the most transformative aspects of my journey was the shift in my mindset. I realized that I had been thinking too small which limited me to my past experiences and beliefs. This shift was paramount in overcoming the barriers that I had been held captive to for so long. I conceptualized a future where my dreams and successes became a tangible reality. I adopted strategies for personal growth, set clear goals, practiced gratitude, and surrounded myself with positive influences. This is what truly provided the sustenance for my garden to flourish.

Reflecting on my life, I see a garden equally balanced with sharp pointed thorns and beautifully bloomed roses. Each chapter of my life has contributed to the person I am today, a woman of resilience, empowerment, and committed to inspiring others. The thorns, while painfully penetrating, have enabled the roses to peak into full bloom all while being mindful that the pain shall pass, and that the best is yet to come.

My message to anyone reading this: If I can do it, you certainly can too! No matter where you start or how many obstacles you face, YOU have the power to overcome and create a life you love. Now is the time to tend to your garden, for even amidst the thorns, there is beauty and growth. Let this serve as a kind reminder that your greatest power lies in your ability to persevere and transform adversity into empowerment. Stand in your garden and with the breeze, take in the scent of the roses, for it has the potential to bloom in ways you never imagined.

Cassandra Lambert

C-Love
Trauma Trained Somatic Practitioner & Artist

https://www.facebook.com/CassandraLoveLambert/
https://www.instagram.com/c_love_lambert/
https://cassandralovelambert.com/
https://www.healwithc-love.com/

Cassandra Love Lambert, also known as C-Love, is the visionary guiding women toward transcending trauma and embracing unyielding confidence, fulfillment, and joy. With mastery in Clinical EFT Tapping, Brainspotting, Somatic Attachment Therapy, and Visual and Performing Arts, Cassandra orchestrates transformative healing experiences like no other.

Driven by her own journey through nearly two decades of healing from C-PTSD rooted in sexual abuse, Cassandra is on a relentless mission to liberate trauma survivors from the chains of their past. With her transformative Sparkle Face and Body Art touching over 15,000 lives, she exudes resilience and empowerment.

As a facilitator of women's Tapping circles and the creator of the groundbreaking Gaslighting Series, Cassandra is revered for her ability to spark profound metamorphoses in her 10-week Somatic Pain into Power Process, leaving women feeling lighter, clearer, and infinitely empowered to reclaim their truth and stride boldly into their futures.

Echoes of Choice:
A Journey Through Shadows and Light

By Cassandra Lambert

On a gloomy, overcast day in San Francisco, the weather reflected the storm of emotions raging within me. As I made my way to the clinic, nausea and fear gnawed at me; I knew I didn't want to go through with the abortion. Desperate for reassurance, I called him, hoping he'd talk me out of it. Instead, his words were cold and final: "You better go through with this, and I don't want anything to do with you or any baby." He hung up, leaving me stunned and alone. In my despair, I reached out to a childhood neighbor who offered me a comforting presence. Despite my reluctance, I proceeded with the abortion, overwhelmed by feelings of isolation and uncertainty about my future. Freshly relocated to San Francisco, studying at SF State, and estranged from my mother due to years of volatile disagreements, my world felt like it was crumbling around me.

The weight of shame pressed heavily on me as I sat in the waiting room, where an unsettling quietness hung in the air, palpable enough to cut through. To my surprise, among the faces, I recognized one from a recent fashion show at SF State. When my name was called for the painkiller meds, I obediently took them. Almost immediately, nausea overtook me, leading me to rush to the bathroom to vomit them out. My youth and naivety left me ill-prepared and uninformed about what would come. After what felt like an eternity, I was ushered into a room.

Much of what transpired remains a haze, but certain moments are seared into my memory. The machine was on, revealing the silhouette of the life inside me. Then came the jarring sound of the vacuum and an excruciating pulling sensation. The pain was unbearable; I felt as if a part of me was dying right there on the table. Alone and consumed by both physical and emotional agony, shame enveloped me as I lay in the recovery bed, waiting to go home. I emerged from that experience irrevocably changed, feeling as though a piece of me had been lost forever, never to return.

Recovery was a slow, somber journey through one of the darkest periods of my life. With dreams of motherhood and a romanticized vision of enduring love, I yearned for the kind of lifelong commitment I had seen in my godfather and his high school sweetheart. Instead, I felt discarded, worthless, and unlovable, questioning whether anyone would ever want me, let alone share a life and a child with me. My roommates were my saving grace during this tumultuous time, cooking for me and tending to my needs. However, the reality of financial pressures soon hit us all, as our involvement in the MLM, Excell, proved insufficient for sustaining our living expenses.

In our quest to find alternative sources of income, we explored various avenues, from pursuing modeling gigs to dedicating ourselves full-time to the MLM business. Eventually, we stumbled upon the idea of working in the gentlemen's clubs of San Francisco. Barely recovered from the

physical and emotional trauma of my recent abortion and the rejection from my ex, I found myself thrust into this new environment. Auditioning at a small venue that admitted those 18 and up, we soon worked long hours amidst the blaring music. Strangely, the constant hustle and noise provided a temporary respite, allowing me to momentarily escape the relentless cycle of thoughts about the painful experience I had just endured.

Working in the gentlemen's clubs of San Francisco became an outlet for my pent-up anger, frustration, and resentment toward men. The years of abuse and betrayal I had suffered at the hands of various men had left deep scars. My sister's father had sexually abused me for years, another had torn me away from my mother and into foster care, and my first love had shattered my heart with his deceit. Each subsequent relationship seemed to confirm my belief that there were no good men out there, only those driven by insatiable sexual desires and a lack of control.

In this job, I found a way to turn my pain into profit, using their weaknesses to my advantage. I believed that by taking their money, I was reclaiming my power, a counterbalance to the years of exploitation and lies I had endured. Initially, this approach worked in my favor, providing me with financial stability and independence. I secured my own place, bought a new car, and transferred from SF State to the Fashion Institute of Design and Merchandising. I even enrolled in an intense Meisner acting class with Rachel Adler, which opened the door to deeper transformation and healing.

As I delved further into personal development through PSI Seminars and engaged in volunteer work, I was able to support my sister as she completed her GED and started her first job. This newfound financial security lifted the burden of constant financial struggle that I had grown accustomed to and desperately wanted to escape. However, the blessings that came with this job came at a significant cost, trapping me in a cycle that would take a decade to transcend.

Despite the positive changes and opportunities unfolding in my life, I found myself ensnared in relationships with abusive, manipulative men. The combination of my traumatic upbringing and the nature of my current 'work' left me convinced that I deserved such mistreatment, resigning myself to the belief that this was simply the harsh reality of life.

Amidst this chaotic backdrop, an unexpected opportunity arose: the chance to donate my eggs to couples struggling with infertility. Driven by the lingering guilt and shame from my past abortion, I felt a deep-seated calling to undertake this endeavor. Over the course of two years, I assisted two families by donating between 20 to 30 eggs. However, during the second round of donations, a medical error resulted in my hospitalization. Enduring unbearable pain, I was connected to a machine that allowed me to self-administer morphine at the press of a button.

Fearing that this experience had robbed me of the chance to have children in the future, I couldn't envision starting a family, given the state of my life at that time.

Sometimes, hitting rock bottom and facing a total loss of options is what it takes to instigate profound life changes. What initially felt like reclaiming my power from men gradually morphed into a suffocating trap. The very avenue that allowed me to transform my pain into profit began to erode my soul, reinforcing the traumas of my childhood. I felt like I was slowly dying inside and desperately needed an escape. I was trapped in a job I loathed, a dancer at gentlemen's clubs since my early twenties. Fueled by the hurt and betrayal I had experienced with men, coupled with the emotional turmoil of an abortion without support, I harbored deep-seated anger and resentment toward them. Their reckless behavior, lack of sexual control, and the constant feelings of being used had pushed me to the edge. I believed that becoming a dancer was my ticket to reclaiming the power stripped from me by life's injustices. However, it soon became clear that this was not the path to empowerment but rather a snare that ensnared me deeper into a cycle that seemed impossible to break free from.

Tears would stream down my face as I drove home, tossing the money I had earned onto the floor as if it were tainted, blood money from a wounded soul. I found myself sobbing in the bathroom at work, seeking solace in alcohol to numb the pain. But as time went on, even alcohol couldn't drown out the overwhelming emotions and the toxic environment that mirrored the very characteristics of men I had come to despise and that had caused me so much anguish. For a decade, I was an exotic dancer, trapped in a cycle I didn't know how to escape. The lifestyle I was living and the income it provided were how I supported myself, put myself through school, and cared for my younger sister without the constant struggle of our impoverished upbringing with a single mother. I was determined never to return to that life of hardship.

Yet, these environments only deepened my internal wounds surrounding relationships and love, perpetuating and reinforcing my childhood traumas I had endured. Unsurprisingly, I couldn't truly heal at a foundational level while still immersed in this lifestyle.

It's no surprise that I found myself in a relationship with someone who deceived me at every turn. I trusted his promises and was eager to break free from the suffocating job and environment that had been sapping my spirit, so I turned a blind eye to the warning signs. Disregarding my better judgment, I packed my belongings, gave away my possessions, and moved with him to LA, only to uncover his web of deceit. Far from having a business or stable income, he was dependent on his mother and friends to support him financially. Once I arrived, it became clear that my savings would be the new funding source for the responsibilities he had assured me he would handle.

My undeserved trust was shattered when I stumbled upon pornographic images he had taken with his camera at an event, revealing a side of him I hadn't known existed. To make matters worse, he abused my dog to the point where she developed severe anxiety and began urinating indoors. Trapped in this toxic relationship, I endured his gaslighting and manipulation, forced to mask my emotions whenever we were around his family and friends. Ashamed of my impulsive decision to move, I felt too embarrassed to seek help.

After enduring eight grueling months, I finally contacted my family for help. My savings were depleted, I had gained weight, and I had given away all my belongings. Feeling utterly shattered and lost, I started life anew from square one. Returning to my mother's house, I reluctantly stepped back into the familiar yet dreaded role of a dancer, this time at a more upscale club. Despite my attempts to break free from this line of work, it felt as though the more I resisted, the tighter its grip became. Faced with this reality, I surrendered to my circumstances, embracing my role at this luxurious club with its showgirl ambiance. After experiencing eight months of hell in that relationship, I was so grateful to get out and become independent again. This newfound feeling associated with this line of work ultimately helped me transcend this job and close this chapter for good due to using it as the vehicle and tool to move forward in life. It lost its weight and power over me.

Concurrently, a friend I had met through PSI Seminars was struggling to cover her expenses and debt, so I introduced her to the world of dancing as a source of income. She embraced it wholeheartedly, diving in with enthusiasm. In return, she introduced me to a new world I had never known: Burning Man. She spoke of this annual event with such passion that it piqued my curiosity. Together, we attended business seminar after seminar, driven by a hunger to learn and desperate to find a way out of dancing.

Despite having no clear business idea or direction, I was irresistibly drawn to investing in the next class, workshop, retreat, or seminar and working with the next coach or mentor. This pursuit became an addiction, fueling an endless search for something more, something better, something different within the realms of healing and personal development. I yearned for a new life, to break free from my past, and to help others along the way.

The opportunity to support an art installation at EDC presented itself, and I eagerly accepted it. This experience introduced me to the world of festivals, the use of substances like molly, and a new level of consciousness I had never encountered before. I met artists and individuals who were unlike anyone I had ever known—more spiritual, more magical, and more aligned with a different way of thinking.

I had just gotten out of an abusive relationship with a pathological liar and sociopath. During this tumultuous period, a gift that had long lain dormant within me resurfaced: the ability to see and

know things. The manifestation of lies became visible on my ex as sores around his mouth, a physical symbol of his deceit exposed for all to see. Breaking free from this toxic relationship, and then experiencing Burning Man for the first time felt like a profound rebirth in many respects.

Burning Man ignited a profound transformation within me, reigniting my inner artist and creativity while reconnecting me with my intuition and ability to flow and manifest. During my first experience at the burn, I witnessed instant manifestations and underwent deep healing on multiple levels. At my second burn, I was gifted the name C-Love, which later evolved into both my artist name and company name.

I became enamored with this vibrant community, where I learned about abundance, the priceless value of creativity, and the possibility of making a living doing what you love—creating art. This incredible community planted beautiful seeds of inspiration and supported me through significant life transitions. They continue to stand by me, and I am forever grateful to have found my soul family.

A new tradition emerged of attending Burning Man each year, followed by Principia with PSI Seminars. At Principia, the universe brought me face-to-face with a soul that felt incredibly kindred—a magnetic connection that was undeniable that year. Vibrating at a higher frequency from my recent Burning Man experience, the pull between us was unshakeable. It felt like a divinely orchestrated meeting, yet it wasn't destined to be a lifetime connection. Someone who had been there every year at the same event however, we didn't meet until this year.

In hindsight, I received my greatest gift through this profound encounter—not a lifetime partner, but a lifetime buddy, my daughter. This relationship marked the first time I experienced something somewhat normal and healthy in a relationship in my life. However, it wasn't equipped to withstand the intense alchemical process of healing and confronting deep-seated wounds, especially as I discovered I was pregnant. We were both too young and ill-prepared to navigate the challenges that arose from all the unhealed trauma in my past, so he bowed out and left, and I stepped up and embarked on this new journey of becoming a single mom.

I was acutely aware that continuing to dance wouldn't be feasible as my body changed and I gained weight during the pregnancy. Uncertainty loomed over me—I had no clear vision of how everything would unfold. Despite the baby's father's assurances that he would support me through the pregnancy and job transition, a nagging feeling told me he wouldn't follow through. Our on-and-off relationship over the past couple of years hadn't shown the level of commitment necessary for such a life-altering journey. Not to mention his heart wouldn't open in the ayahuasca ceremony we had done together, which gave me a foreboding premonition of him leaving.

Complicating matters further, his family held a harsh judgment of me, solely based on my profession, without considering my journey or the challenges I had overcome. As my body underwent the transformative process of pregnancy, old wounds from my past surged to the surface, placing additional strain on our relationship. Our bond faltered without the necessary tools or support system to navigate these complexities, deepening my uncertainty about the future.

Within a week of a sacred healing ceremony we had shared together with a shaman, he vanished from my life, leaving behind a void of unfulfilled promises and shattered dreams. Discovering my pregnancy at such a crucial juncture, while I was immersed in seeking answers and pursuing change, thrust me into a profound crossroads. I grappled with an agonizing decision: to embrace single motherhood or to terminate the pregnancy. What added layers of complexity to this choice were my past experiences—a history of a prior pregnancy and abortion, coupled with the repercussions of egg donation, which had led to hospitalization due to ovarian overstimulation. These experiences cast a shadow over my present dilemma, amplifying the weight of my decision and the uncertainty of what lay ahead.

This pregnancy was nothing short of a miracle to me—a glimmer of hope amid uncertainty. Yet, it brought forth a haunting question: Could I bear the possibility of never experiencing motherhood if I chose to terminate this pregnancy? The answer reverberated within me—a resounding no. For as long as I could remember, the dream of becoming a mother and having a daughter had been etched deep within my heart. Despite the less-than-ideal circumstances—a lack of a life partner and clarity about my purpose—I knew I couldn't ignore my soul's calling. With unwavering resolve, I took a leap of faith into the unknown and embraced this baby, knowing that this decision would mark one of the most profound blind leaps of faith I have ever taken.

I affectionately refer to my daughter as my answered prayer, my divine intervention. Her presence in my life signifies a pivotal turning point— a moment of clarity that illuminated the path I was meant to walk. Without her, I may have remained trapped in a vocation slowly eroding my soul, pulling me further from the desires of my heart. For years, I had prayed for guidance, yearning for a sign to lead me toward the change I so desperately needed. And when I discovered I was pregnant, it became unmistakably clear: I had to confront the unknown and embrace the transformation I had longed for.

This decision was the most difficult I have ever faced, yet it was also humbling. It required me to leave the comfort of familiarity and venture into uncharted territory. But in doing so, I found a strength within myself that I never knew existed—a resilience born from the willingness to surrender to the unknown and trust in the journey ahead. My daughter, my answered prayer, remains a constant reminder of the power of faith and the profound impact of stepping into the unfamiliar with courage and conviction.

Navigating the complexities of getting aid and welfare was a humbling experience—a journey that stripped away layers of pride and forced me to confront the harsh realities of my circumstances. Moving back to my mother's house, I found myself grappling with feelings of inadequacy and failure. For three long months, I slept on an air mattress on the concrete floor in the family room, surrounded by bags of my belongings, with no privacy or comfort to shield me from the weight of my despair.

Returning to my childhood home reignited old wounds and patterns of relating that I had fled from for so long. The familiar echoes of constant criticism, feeling unsupported and used, and being subjected to overpowering control washed over me again. In this environment, I was constantly placed in a position of fault, with a distinct lack of respect or care for my well-being. My parent's house (which was in a between stage of a remodel) mirrored my internal state—unfinished, stripped to its frame, and haunted by the ghosts of unresolved pain and dysfunction.

Amidst the void of despair, a whisper of intuition pierced through the silence, urging me to take a leap of faith. With nothing to lose, I reached out to someone and asked if I could showcase my art at the back of their event. Though I had only dabbled in face and body art for the past two years at Burning Man, I trusted this inspired idea with unwavering conviction. To my surprise, she agreed, and I hastily set up at Supper Club in San Francisco.

Armed with hand-written signs bearing simple instructions—#1: Say hi, #2: Sit down, #3: Become art—I embarked on what I believed would be a temporary endeavor. Little did I know, this moment marked the genesis of a decade-long business journey. What began as a modest venture soon blossomed into something far more significant, fueled by the tagline "Spreading Love One Brush Stroke at a Time." As my business flourished, it evolved into a movement—a testament to the power of intuition and the transformative potential of following one's inspired ideas.

The dynamic of guilt surrounding my work while simultaneously being expected to contribute financially to childcare was a perplexing and emotionally draining experience. It felt like a constant tug-of-war between being criticized for striving to provide for my daughter and being coerced into financial obligations. The manipulation and conflicting expectations left me feeling disheartened and frustrated.

It took five years of tireless dedication to build my art business to a point where I felt financially secure enough to venture out independently. Moving out of my mother's house and into our own space was a monumental step toward breaking free from the unhealthy familial dynamics that had plagued us for so long. After years of cramped living conditions in a tiny room, transitioning to a spacious two-story townhome was both exhilarating and overwhelming. It took time for us to adjust to the newfound freedom and space, allowing ourselves the opportunity to decompress from the constraints of our past living situation.

During chaos and uncertainty, I birthed two babies simultaneously—my beloved daughter and my flourishing business, C-Love. Both began as humble seeds planted in the fertile soil of possibility and through unwavering dedication and faith, they grew to thrive. This is a testament to the transformative power of taking a leap of faith and heeding guidance from a higher source. Life has a remarkable way of coming full circle when we surrender to its flow.

Now, I devote myself to helping women navigate their journeys of transformation, empowering them to turn their pain into power through my trauma-informed five-stage somatic process. If you're interested in delving deeper into my story and the work I do, keep an eye out for my upcoming solo book, *Into the Light: Becoming My Own Hero*, set to release this September. In it, I'll share more about the trials and triumphs that have shaped my path. For further connection and insight, visit my website at www.CassandraLoveLambert.com or connect with me on Instagram @C_Love_Lambert. Let's embrace the journey of becoming our own heroes and stepping into the light of our true potential.

Marissa Warren

Marissa Warren
Hypnotherapist & Transformational Consultant

https://www.linkedin.com/in/marissawarren-hypnotherapist-transformationalconsultant/
https://www.facebook.com/marissa.warren.transformational
https://www.instagram.com/marissawarren_/
https://www.marissawarren.com/

Marissa is a globally renowned clinical hypnotherapist and transformational consultant working with RTT – Rapid Transformational Therapy, QHHT – Quantum Healing Hypnosis Technique, Somatic and Tantric embodiment, breathwork and sound healing. I am an international speaker and author.

Marissa embodies these modalities in her life and have used these to heal trauma, make major changes, create transformations and align to her soul's and life's purpose.

For those ready to reclaim inner freedom, break free from past limitations, step into their best life, take action, are ready to uplevel and elevate their life, want to achieve true transformations, and realign with their souls' purpose and align to their own unique authenticity and sovereignty – Marissa is the transformational consultant to help!

Leaving you feeling empowered, living from infinite inner power and potential and stepping into the life and level of success you desire. Marissa will help you tap into your inner magic and utilise your inner resources to step up and shine.

Marissa has a phenomenal ability to tap deeply into people's subconscious to help them break free from internal limitations, negative patterns and behaviours and allow them to move into living their dream life and souls purpose.

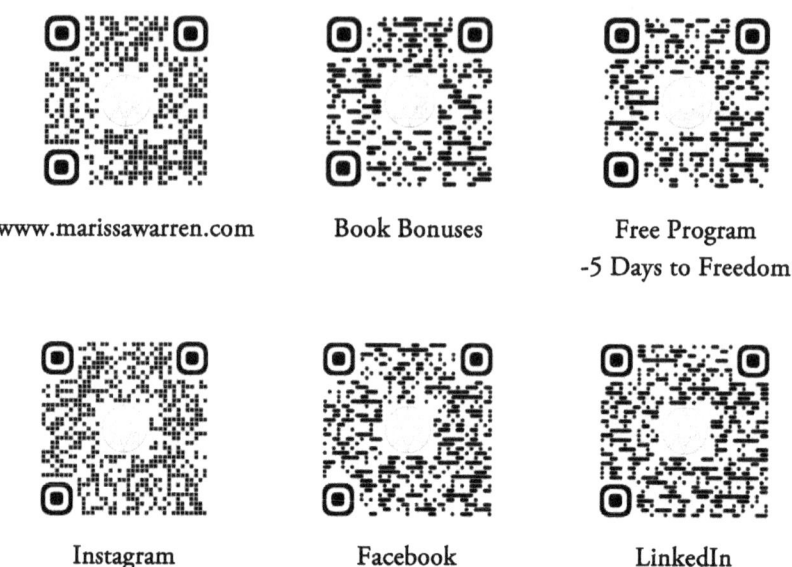

www.marissawarren.com

Book Bonuses

Free Program
-5 Days to Freedom

Instagram

Facebook

LinkedIn

Life Is for Living:
Turning Adversity into Triumph to Live a Life
of Soul Purpose and Passion

By Marissa Warren

There is nothing like death to make you face the realities of mortality...

When I was eight years old, my father was diagnosed for the first time with cancer. It was at this age that I was forced to face the reality of death and that not everyone you love is in your life forever. A big reality to face as a small child. Seeing my father have multiple surgeries and treatments and then not only go on to recover from this cancer, but one more major cancer, only to not be able to beat the third major cancer. At eight years old, I was told my father would die. At this young age, I was facing a life without my father. This event impacted my entire family and my upbringing. He was told by many doctors that he would not live past 6 – 8 months. He defied the odds and went on to live another thirty-two years.

It was through this adversity that I learnt my greatest strengths in life from my father – resilience, determination and the need to always be an advocate for my health.

These traits would not be cemented into me until after a lifetime of experiences. I can now say in 2024, at 44 years old, that I have a high level of respect and appreciation for my life and my body. However, it wasn't always this way. Throughout my younger years, I completely disrespected my body through unhealthy lifestyle choices, excessive partying, and living with this feeling like life was short, so I squeeze as much in as possible – I still feel like this but now create magic moments and enjoy seeing as much of the world as possible. I've had a lot of fun in my life and wouldn't change my life and experiences as this has made me who I am today and led me to the work I am doing now.

When my father passed one week before my 40th birthday, I felt like my whole world imploded. So much stuff that had been buried deep within me came bubbling up to the surface. A lot of generational traumas, unprocessed trauma, long-forgotten and blacked-out traumatic events, fertility challenges, negative relationship choices and unhealthy lifestyle choices all came up to be faced and dealt with.

I finally had no option but to face everything I had been running from, both consciously and subconsciously, my entire life. This was the beginning of a journey that would forever change my life. Doing the deep inner work and diving deep into the abyss of my soul has still been, to date, the most challenging and confronting work I have ever done and the gift of the biggest level of expansion I could ever experience. Now, there is nothing that anyone can say to me or do to me that can even come close to the level of pain that it was to sit in with myself and shine the light on the shadow aspects that had been lying dormant, but had been powerfully impacting my life and running the show.

My deep healing journey wasn't a quick fix or one specific action that soothed my soul. It was a combination of different healing modalities, doing the work that I do with my clients myself and packing up my house and going on a deep soul journey travelling through South America for 4.5 months. I journeyed on a deep inward soul discovery and reconnection in Costa Rica, met soul connections, sat with shamans, had private ceremonies in the mountains in Peru, connected back to nature in the Galapagos and the Amazon in Ecuador, experienced the diversity in Bolivia, chilled out in Colombia, stargazed in Chile and got soaked under the Iguazu Falls in Argentina, danced every day and deeply connected to my feminine energy in Brazil, pushed myself in ways that I had never before and opened myself up to the unknown along the way. I also went all in with the modalities that I now use with my clients. I believe that you can only take others to the depth that you have journeyed yourself, and I have been deep in the trenches of life and healing, many times.

There is a real power in owning your story without being your story. When you can get to a point where you have healed enough from the situation to be able to talk about it in a way that it no longer owns you, takes over your mind, body or emotional state and can learn from the experience and meet it with forgiveness and compassion, your pain becomes your superpower.

I am forever appreciative and grateful for all the experiences in my life: the good, the bad and the painful. Without these, I wouldn't be the person I am today, which is someone with a deep level of empathy and compassion and a mission to help elevate the global consciousness and to empower others to access and tap into their own inner magic and innate healing abilities. I would love to see as many people as possible, become less reliant on external fixes and solutions and more empowered to be able to listen to their intuition, live a life that is aligned truly to them, live a life of soul purpose and passion and access their own inner healing and transformative elements. Life is for living, and I believe that we are all worthy and deserving of living our best life and have the inner capabilities to achieve our dreams.

The work I am doing is truly my life purpose and my legacy to the world. I am in awe daily of the phenomenal results that my clients achieve, and the best part is, I am the guide along the journey, the cheerleader on the sidelines and the archaeologist helping to uncover what needs to be released to be healed and it is the client that is achieving these amazing results – all from being able to access deeper and different parts of themselves. Everything we need to know and understand, to shift and change, to release and evolve is already within us, sometimes we just need a little help to access this.

Hi, I'm Marissa. I am a globally renowned clinical hypnotherapist and transformational consultant working with RTT – Rapid Transformational Therapy, QHHT – Quantum Healing Hypnosis Technique, PTSD Hypnotherapy, Somatic and Tantric embodiment, breathwork and sound healing. I am also an international speaker and author.

I truly embody these modalities in my daily life and have used these myself to heal from trauma, make major life changes, create lasting transformations and align with my soul's purpose. This work is truly the work I am here to do, and it is my life's purpose. I now use these modalities with my clients to help them break free from past limitations and live their best lives.

I aim to leave my clients feeling empowered, living from their infinite inner power and potential and stepping into the life and level of success they truly desire. Everything you need is already within you, and I will help to tap into this inner magic and utilise the inner resources to step up and shine.

Rapid Transformational therapy is a fantastic modality created by Marisa Peer. Combing hypnosis, cognitive behavioural therapy, NLP – neuro linguistic programming and psychotherapy together to really get to the root cause of whatever is going on and creating an issue or limitation in life, then release this and then recode and rewire the subconscious to operate in a more aligned and conducive way to help move the client into living the life they have always wanted to live and to create the life they truly desire. It's super effective for achieving amazing results. I often find clients that come to me after trying it all, they've seen everyone and spent countless hours in therapy, counselling and are at their last resort. The thing I love the most about this work is the changes that occur and ripple out into many areas of life. This is a super effective treatment and whereas normal hypnotherapy may require 4 – 6 or more sessions for an issue or area of concern, the method of RTT can achieve deeper results in 1 – 3 sessions. This is due to the therapy modalities used during hypnosis.

QHHT is working with past life regression and is the Dolores Cannon Method. There is so much that can be carried through, which can all impact health and harmony in this current and daily life. By accessing deeper parts of yourself, it helps to gain a deeper understanding into you and allows you to tap into the inner wisdom of YOU! This can be a great modality to release past karma or burdens and go on a deeper inner journey of self-exploration. This is a phenomenal option for those seeking their life purpose – knowing that there is a deep feeling of wanting more from life and knowing that you are destined for more in this life.

PTSD Hypnotherapy uses clinical hypnotherapy to help eliminate PTSD-type symptoms. With the heightened stress levels of daily life, most people, if not all, have experienced some level and degree of trauma, so this method works not just for PTSD symptoms, but also for trauma of varying degrees.

I incorporate the **somatic and tantric embodiment, breathwork and sound healing** in the container that I work intensively together with my clients. These are lifetime-lasting resources and real-life practical skills to implement into daily life moving forward to provide emotional regulation and equilibrium.

The offerings of modalities that I provide have proven results and have been combined to maximise the results and provide long-lasting benefits and transformations.

Each element works differently but also in conjunction with each other to accelerate and expedite the results and to empower the client to be able to implement these resources and tools into other areas of their life.

I love working with my clients, but I also love to see them empowered and ready to move on from whatever has been holding them back. I absolutely love to help my clients make change easy and to bypass the years and hard work that it took me to be able to align with my life's purpose and live the life I always wanted to live. This work that I am doing is truly the work I am here to do and my legacy. I know that there is an easier way and I can help others bio hack their way there too, making change easier and faster. Success leaves clues and when you follow the experts and implement the proven strategies, it is easier to emulate the results in a shorter amount of time.

Change comes from change and it is through the incremental, daily shifts and habitual layer stacking that those big changes manifest. There is no magical quick fix, healing isn't a linear journey and the path looks different for everyone.

I am the transformational consultant for those ready to reclaim inner freedom, step into living life on their own terms, take action and do the work to make lasting and deep changes, are ready to uplevel and elevate their life, want to achieve true transformations, and realign with their souls' purpose while aligning to their own unique authenticity and sovereignty.

If you are ready to move through your current plateau and elevate your life – I am the transformational consultant for you!

I am the solution for those that have tried everything but are still not where they want to be. I help to access your inner wisdom and infinite potential to be empowered to make changes and gain a deeper insight into yourself and your life. What clients come to see me for and what they leave with is far more than they ever expected. If you are ready to do the inner work and be guided and supported along the journey, I am here to help!

With a wealth of knowledge and experience, I am the go-to for expert advice, insights, mindset, motivation and inspiration. I can tap into and access deeper parts of yourself and have an acute level of understanding over the "why" of people, their behaviours, motivators and how to achieve lasting levels of transformation.

The areas of expertise I specialise in are:

- Abundance mindset and strategies
- Addictions
- Athletes / Sports performance
- Birth / Conception / Fertility
- Breaking ancestral trauma and generational bonds
- Business Owners – increase success, move to higher levels of performance
- Confidence
- Financial – sabotages and wealth increases
- Healing past trauma
- Health Issues

- Imposter syndrome
- Insomnia
- Life Purpose
- Motivational mindset / procrastination
- Relationships
- Self-Esteem / Self-Value / Self-Worth
- Sexual addictions / Disorders / Dysfunctions
- Stress
- Success Strategies
- Weight

To help as many people as possible, my first book, *Elevate; Make change easy to transform your* is filled with practical insights, tools and techniques to help you transform your life and move from where you are to where you want to be. This is the book that I wished that I had at so many points in my life to help me cement in the changes I was trying to make. Elevate also includes my signature somatic codes of the body and life formula. These have been curated to help you on the psychospiritual level and align you to your life's purpose. Enjoy your copy by scanning the QR code.

Order Elevate Book

If this work sounds like something that you need in your life and you are ready to elevate, if you need help diving into yourself on a deeper level, want to break free from your internal limitations, then please reach out. I offer a free discovery call where we can meet and discuss what is going on for you and the best treatment plan to help you move into the life you want to be living. You are worthy and deserving of living your best life.

BOOK FREE DISCOVERY CALL

Shakti Rios

The PHNX Legacy
Mentor & Healer

https://facebook.com/phnxshakti
https://instagram.com/phnx_shakti
https://phnxlegacy.com

Shakti Rios, a certified Human Design Business & Career Analyst & IEFT (Instructional EFT) & Emotional Freedom Technique (EFT) Practitioner, is a guiding light for those seeking alignment & embodied success.

With 14 years of entrepreneurial experience in healing, trauma resolution, and spiritual advancement, she empowers individuals to embrace their unique path & align with their success algorithm. Shakti's transformative approach fuses Human Design and multidimensional healing modalities to liberate clients from mental and emotional limitations, paving the way for authentic success.

She firmly believes that inherent genius resides in everyone, and her work is dedicated to helping clients unlock their true potential. Shakti Rios is more than an entrepreneur; she's a transformational guide.

Her mission is clear: to unlock the cosmic genius within each individual, fostering a world where fulfilled and empowered souls radiate their true brilliance.

Handed the Short Stick:
Choice In Adversity

By Shakti Rios

I was born and died the same week.

You could imagine the setup this gives a kid in terms of their relationship to reality. *Yeesh.*

I have a running joke that I came into this world, realized what a shit show it was, and quickly pressed the red button to get the hell out. I imagine It was at that point that God lovingly nudged me back into my body and asked me to have the courage to see this thing out.

For the most part, I'm grateful that I agreed. *For the most part…*

So, this was my beginning. Having crossed through the veil of death right at the beginning of life leaves you with a certain openness in your psyche. Not unlike the myriad of Near Death Experiences you read about where people crossover and come back a *little* different.

When this happens to you, you're not quite as tied into the matrix of this world. You're *different* forever after that. It has often felt like I was a walking alien just existing amongst humans and trying to do my best to be one.

As extraordinary as the beginning of my life was, my family's origin is equally as extraordinary.

As Cuban refugees, they fled in the late 70s to the US avoiding the absolute horror show that became of their country once Castro took power. At the time of leaving, my maternal grandparents had already served over 15 years of prison combined for "crimes against the government," and my mother had served in a "work camp" for years (*read: concentration camp where young kids were separated from their parents and forced to work farmlands for the government while living in shacks unattended),* then married very young to her first love and had a 4-month baby (my older brother) on the plane to the US. *They lost everything.* They showed up in a foreign country with no money, no language, and an infant.

These were the remarkable humans that raised me. Resilient doesn't even begin to cut it.

Being the ONLY one of my immediate family born in this new land came with its own set of trials. I didn't learn English until I was about 6. I honestly didn't realize there was a world outside of my culture until about then either. I worked HARD to be noticed, stand out, and be seen as remarkable. I had this unspoken knowing that I lived riding the coattails of literal revolutionaries and their sacrifice became the momentum I swung with to scale higher and higher educationally and professionally. I was wired to excel and have/do everything they didn't/couldn't.

More than anything, they wanted me to follow a very straight and narrow path to what they thought would be a success for me and to *please, please, please* not kill myself in the process of doing that.

And then around my teens, the wheels came off, and that was when I started to recognize - *I was different.* Not just a little different, VERY different.

I could hear, see, and know things that others couldn't. And while this was a phenomenon that happened all through my childhood it wasn't until this age that I started understanding with clarity what this meant.

Shortly after those years I found my way into deep metaphysical studies, mind/body healing, and deep mysticism and recognized that there was much more to the reality I could "see" than I thought. My early 20s felt like a literal renaissance.

My studies led me into deep experimentation with my own body and with the limits of reality. I started questioning my narrative of being "sick" and having to tread lightly. I began using meditation, frequency, and other self-hypnosis techniques to maintain health and stamina. Every time I returned for a medical checkup I left all the technicians and physicians stunned - somehow, despite going against all their recommendations, I was thriving. They labeled me an anomaly and let it go.

Except I knew I WASN'T an anomaly.

Yes, I was different.

AND, somehow I knew that everything I was capable of doing *anyone* was capable of, also.

It became really apparent to me that very FEW people actually believe in their own capacity to heal, create, manifest, or live happily. I observed a sort of spell over most of humanity that created a sleepy, half-hearted experience of life mostly surrounded by different numbing agents and steeped in massive repetitive negative beliefs.

At 24, I became a massage therapist and pursued that career for nearly a decade. This work put me in so many different rooms with wildly different humans and I began to understand the impact that psychology had on the body. It was through the messaging in my hands that I understood that we are in fact entirely connected and that issues that live in tissues and tissues (like hips!) don't lie.

Many life events between that fateful decade as a massage therapist and now, further corroborated on this learning that body/mind/spirit are an intricate network in a very nuanced symbiotic relationship. When one is grossly out of balance, the others will also automatically be. They rely on each other.

This expounds on the ancient spiritual understanding that "as above, so below."

In the same way, we live on a globe that is an ecosystem in intimate relationships with all manner of life, so are the different aspects of us (aura, body, emotions, thoughts…) also in an intimate and nuanced relationship with each other. We are the microcosm of this magnificent world.

With the advent of quantum physics and the outrageous amount of insight we've been able to glean about our interaction with the consciousness field, we now also understand that we are infinitely entangled with everything AND everyone in EVERY way. What happens on one side of the world DOES affect the other at a subatomic and sometimes NOT so subatomic level.

To understand this more visually, think of Professor Charles Xavier (lovingly called Professor X) from the classic show *X-men*. He has this machine he named Cerebro. When he puts on the helmet that acts like a transmitter, the giant screen in front of him produces the precise location of any mutant he wishes to locate. This machine allows his consciousness to immediately tap into the consciousness of every mutant around the world. With this technology, he is able to find anyone he needs to in the mutant community. That metaphor is not too far off for how we are all wired to each other.

This is impactful beyond immediate comprehension.

This means that TRULY we could be entangled with ANYONE or any CIRCUMSTANCE that has happened in our lives at ANY point - *past, present, OR future*. Because time is NON linear and it is in fact all happening simultaneously there is the capacity to be living out in a sort of "glitch" because of a situation that occurred on a different time plane than the one you are currently living in.

THIS understanding changes the way you look at the world, your experiences in the "past" and what is happening currently in your reality.

Have you ever wondered why you seem to repeat the same patterns over and over again?

Dating the same asshole.

Ending up at the same dead-end jobs.

Always broke no matter HOW much money you make.

Can't lose weight even though you feel like you're doing all the things.

Our experiences are affected far beyond what we think in this material reality. We are first and foremost - energy beings. The way of creation is energy FIRST - then matter. Energy FORMS matter.

When we are considering adjusting to change or actively creating it - we have to understand the ORDER by which change happens: energy first, then matter. Thoughts/Feelings FIRST then Result.

Thoughts + Feelings = Result/Consequence.

Did your long-term relationship just end? Backtrack on the thoughts and feelings you or they were having for at least a few months to a few years.

Are you struggling to lose weight? Backtrack to WHY you don't want to lose it and the fear underlying it suddenly not being there. What's the payoff you are receiving for NOT losing it?

Did you just get fired? Backtrack to how much you wanted out of that job deep down and WHY you wanted out.

You will find that this pattern always proves true.

First, there is thought + feeling and then there is the following consequence. *Please note that this happens on a collective level, also.*

In the same way that WE can generate momentum with our thoughts/feelings to affect ourselves - the same thing can happen to affect larger communities & countries.

The unrest seen around the globe is a consequence of momentum. The momentum of a few turned to many that have a vested interest in the unrest existing. If there wasn't an interest and a pointed desire for it - *it wouldn't exist.* Matter cannot exist without energy.

So the question collectively is - *where is the energy for that unrest coming from?* That's a whole lot of a conversation for another book. But the same concept we are exploring individually applies collectively.

What I inherently understood, as a child born with a crippling diagnosis that should've killed me but didn't, is that we are more than just a statistic or a happenstance.

Statistically, I shouldn't be alive.

Statistically, I should've had multiple surgeries all of my life to keep up with my growth.

Statistically, I should've never been able to bring two children to life with a vaginal delivery.

Statistically, I should've not been able to be a fitness coach for five years at peak performance lifting heavy weights.

Every statistic that was thrown at me, I shattered.

Not because I am magical, but because I didn't accept the *construct* (energy) I was being fed.

Whereas the thoughts and feelings of others ABOUT me were clouded in fear, illness, and concern - I thought of myself as strong, capable, and resilient.

Whenever I was met with a belief by a doctor or my parents regarding what I was or was not able to do, I discarded it abruptly and replaced it with something I wanted to believe about myself and my abilities.

I focused on meditation, nourishing my body well, and movement. As I studied and was certified in different healing modalities for the nervous system and emotional regulation, I applied all that as well.

My focus became *how I perceived myself* and felt about myself first and foremost and then I worked on the physical aspects.

The result has been a very robust and vital life that was not happenstance - *it was the knowing that energy precedes matter.* By the grace of God, I was given a chance to exist, which I recognize as a massive privilege already.

With that grace that I was extended, I chose to build on it daily with more grace and more practices that enhanced my own well-being against the better judgment of those overseeing my care.

I am not an anomaly despite what everyone said.

There are countless documented cases of regular people overcoming WILD physical adversity despite the best physicians/educators around them telling them they would NOT and could NOT survive it.

Look no further than the now very famous thought leader, Dr. Joe Dispenza. After a crippling biking accident that left him paralyzed from the next down and told he would NEVER walk or move again - he reversed the negative impacts of that incident using the same principles I have just shared in this short passage.

We are extraordinary beings.

Truly, our potential is limited only to our capacity to harness it.

If you are currently traversing a pivot in your life that feels completely terrifying and destabilizing - understand that you have so much power here.

No other being on this planet has the capacity to tell YOU how you get to live or experience your life.

Every statistic is a wild fucking guess and doesn't have to define you. Allow yourself the true grace of knowing this and living EVERY day of your life with this in your back pocket.

Pursue EVERY avenue that empowers you and enhances your mental fortitude and emotional resilience.

For you are made of the same stars that decorate our Universe and thereby are endowed with the same magnetic power they are.

With great love for all you are and all you get to be,
Shakti

Marlene Gravenberch

Founder of Leadership Refocused

https://www.linkedin.com/in/marlene-gravenberch-5655a61a
https://www.facebook.com/MMIGravenberch
https://www.instagram.com/marlenegravenberch
https://leadership-refocused.com

Born and raised in Suriname, Marlène wears many hats in her personal life—mom, grandma, aunt, cousin, and even a sister to her sisters-of-another-mother!

In July 2023, she took a big step and started her own coaching business. Her focus is on empowering leaders, especially women. Reflecting on her life, Marlène realizes she always had that coaching DNA within her, shaped by her role as the oldest among her siblings and cousins on her mom's side.

From an early age, Marlène knew she wanted to become a teacher. Educating and empowering others has been the common thread in her life, and it set the tone for her mission: to ignite possibilities, foster excellence, and create environments where everyone can unlock their full leadership potential. Marlène believes in unlocking the full leadership potential within each person and empowering their journey towards success, especially for women. She has shown her expertise in personal and professional development through her work in various organizations, and she's passionate about helping people grow and succeed, both personally and professionally.

In April 2024, Marlène teamed up with two other coaches to host a workshop called ""Reinvent Yourself: Reset to Evolve."" As part of promoting the workshop, she had her first-time appearance on national TV (STVS) and twice on local radio (Radio 10). Other significant events for Marlène in her professional life are: being a guest on Marissa Warren's podcast 'Elevate with Marissa' (March 2024) and being on SRS Podcast Interview (August 2024).

Besides personal and professional coaching, she also supports local businesses and startups with their operational processes and policies. For now, she offers these services locally and mostly in person.

Marlène has faced challenges when she worked in male-dominated environments and often being the only woman in the management team. There was even a situation where a male colleague expressed his dislike for her simply because she wanted to mediate between him and the CEO, when she was the HR Manager there.

On a personal level, Marlène struggled for nearly 30 years to maintain a relationship, trying to fix herself and her partner, while she was getting more broken. In 2013, she came to the crossroad, where she told herself to make a decision that would bring her peace. This journey is for another book! 😊

If she hadn't grown personally, Marlène wouldn't have been able to handle these experiences in a healthy way.

When Marlène is not enjoying family time, sipping wine with close friends, enjoying nature, reading books or listening to different genres of music, you'll often find her helping as a volunteer by being an active member on the board of The Prasoro Foundation (a Foster Home for children), Coaching young adults in different areas of their interest, Coaching/ mentoring students in thesis writing, and do free coaching sessions with women to empower and elevate them.

For further insights into Marlène and the ways she can support you in personal and professional development, explore her expertise at https://leadership-refocused.com

My Journey of Forgiveness

By Marlene Gravenberch

Forgiveness is not an easy road, as I have experienced. It is about the slow, tough journey through your own emotions, forgiving others and—forgiving yourself. This journey took me through all sorts of emotions until I found peace and healing.

My Journey

My journey of forgiveness started when it finally hit me that I may not grow old with the one I deeply loved, my then-husband, because of his infidelity lots of times. All these years, I have hung onto the relationship because I could not see my life without him.

For the outside world, our relationship looked great, everything seemed okay (happy couple and being this long in a relationship). It is not common in our family to be this long (almost 30 years) in a relationship, and if you are, it is at all cost.

The year before I turned 50 (in 2013), I was at a crossroads, making a choice if I could live this lie for the rest of my life, being hurt, angry, sad, almost feeling like I was slowly dying…

I had all these mixed emotions because I sometimes was happy after my then-husband promised to change and it did not happen. Telling myself that was his only flaw (infidelity). I told myself that other women were in worse situations compared to me, like he was not hitting me, not knowing I was downplaying my own situation.

In 2013, I looked at myself in the mirror and asked myself: *"Marlène, will you end up like your mom, slowly dying of heartbreak and grief?"* Every time I discovered he was cheating, my heart got broken again, losing more and more self-confidence.

Angry at myself, I felt like I had failed everyone: my family, especially our children, causing them sadness, although they were adults if I chose to separate from their dad. I also felt fear: Where will I live? I don't want to move in with family or friends; move on <u>alone and be on my own</u>.

I am a believer and I started praying, *"How will I be able to face these fears and mixed emotions?"* I had nowhere to go, even if I wanted to get out of this relationship, and I was so angry because that is what I was focusing on, feeling more desperate and I got angrier. And, in that anger, it was like I heard a voice: **If you don't forgive, I cannot open doors for you! You have to forgive him, in order to move on.**

I was astonished because I felt that I had been wronged, and yet I had to forgive. I screamed in anger and frustration to the Lord: *"Why??? Why me??? What is this, Lord??? What are you asking from me!! How can I do this???"* I felt stuck because I did not know how to do this painful forgiveness thing.

I shared this experience with my then-HR Assistant who is very religious and an elder in her church. She talked to me about forgiveness from the Bible perspective and encouraged me to start learning more about forgiveness, not only from the Bible perspective but also the whole process around it.

I started reading about forgiveness and the process, and I discovered that this is something very personal. For me, I had to try to understand my then-husband's motives, why he could not stay faithful. I listened to his arguments, trying to place them in perspective, still feeling this anger. I wanted to see for myself what my part was in his arguments because he did not want to let me go, yet he couldn't promise to stay faithful.

I shared with him that I decided that in our relationship, being faithful is a non-negotiable for me. Every time it hurt too much to discover the infidelity. It was during that process I also learned that I had to set my boundaries and my non-negotiable for other relationships. It was during that process I learned how important it is that you know at an early age what your core values are, to develop a sound relationship with yourself, and then you can set your boundaries. I started writing about this for myself.

My Stages of Forgiveness

1. Denial, Heartbreak, Desperation, and Anger: It usually starts here.

    - Denial acts like a buffer—it keeps the full impact of the hurt at bay, for me it was comparing my situation with other women, telling myself the only flaw my then-husband had was his infidelity.
    - Heartbroken and physically feeling sick, not being able to get out of bed, wanting to just curl up and not being able to eat. I had to force myself out of bed to go to work and to eat something. Here is also where I felt the grief as if someone had died and part of me died too.
    - Desperation, especially if you have (little) children and nowhere to go.
    - Anger, raw and fiery, is a response to the pain and betrayal you feel. You might find yourself yelling, complaining to friends, or just simmering quietly. It is all part of the process. I went through all these emotions.

2. Acknowledgment and Acceptance:

    - It is tough admitting you are hurt and even tougher to let yourself feel it all.
    - But herc is the deal: acceptance is not about saying what happened was okay. It is about saying your feelings are valid. It is about owning up to the hurt and standing firm in your right

to feel it. That is where I know I had to learn more about this forgiveness process to accept what has happened to me and that feeling all the mixed emotions is part of this process.

3. Empathy and Understanding:

- This might sound like a stretch now, but with time, you might start seeing things from the other person's point of view. As mentioned earlier, I wanted to understand the motives for this infidelity.

- This is not about excusing them but understanding the offender is human too, messed up as anyone else. Maybe they were under pressure, had their own issues, or just made a bad choice. It does not excuse it, but it helps explain it. Although I understand and still do not agree, for me it was part of the process. In my case, my then-husband was like *"I love you! You are the one! Having a one-night stand or a short-term relationship will not change that. I will never leave you."* He wouldn't let me go.

4. Letting Go and Release:

- This is the biggie. Letting go means easing up on the resentment and the bitterness. It is not about forgetting or pretending nothing happened. It is about deciding not to let those feelings rule your life.

- This step is freeing, like setting down a heavy load you have been carrying way too long. This is where I decided to still have the (grand)father of my (grand)children to be part of my life in a healthy and friendly relationship.

5. Peace and Healing:

- The last part of the journey. This is when you find your calm. The hurt hasn't vanished yet, but it does not control you anymore. You are stronger, wiser, and yes, even happier. Peace comes from accepting the past, letting it shape but not confine you, finding ways to live with it, and moving on.

- Don't underestimate this last part. This is a step-by-step process because there will be triggers that will bring up some or more of the emotions but that will become less and less. My whole forgiveness journey took me almost two and a half years.

How Do You Know You Have Totally Forgiven Your Offender?

Here are a few signs:

- Lighter Heart: You feel like a weight has been lifted from your shoulder and chest.
- Empathy: You can see their side of things, without saying it was okay.
- Less Resentment: The bitterness begins to fade, leaving room for peace.
- Moving On: You don't feel stuck in the past anymore.
- Self-Compassion: You are kind to yourself, acknowledging your own worth and struggles.
- Freedom: You feel liberated, no longer trapped by anger, grief, or hurt.

What Helped Me Through This Journey

1. Praying: Offered me both spiritual comfort and practical benefits and served as a way to connect with my higher power, which provided a sense of guidance and peace when I dealt with the complex emotions associated with forgiveness.
2. Journaling: I wrote it all out and this helped me sort through my feelings and find some clarity.
3. Seeking Support: I had a small support group to talk to. One

person who truly helped me through this process was Mrs. Uselene Vrede, my then-HR Assistant (as mentioned earlier). She prayed with and for me. We worked together for 5 years, so she observed and experienced my whole process up close and personal.

4. Practicing Mindfulness: Noticing my thoughts and feelings without judgment.

What Came Out of This for Me?

- Most importantly, I was able to forgive my then-husband for myself, and myself for feeling that I had failed to keep this relationship going but also for being angry at myself.
- Identifying my core values, rediscovering myself and what I stand for in developing a relationship with myself.
- Learning to enjoy my own company—unlearning the incomplete feeling without a partner and the need for the constant company of someone else.
- Learning to share my feelings and set healthy boundaries.
- Being at peace with myself from within and developing a high sense of self-love.
- Understanding other's points of view and asking curious questions.
- Still creating space in my heart for a future partner with whom I share the same values. I did not become a *manhater*.
- In my forgiving process, I decided to choose to stay in a healthy and friendly relationship with the father of my kids. Together, we can be at birthday parties, have trips together with other family members, and we are there for each other.
- Last but not least: indeed, lots of doors opened. I was blessed with higher-paid jobs and I was able to buy a house I now live in since 2017.

- I founded my own company, Leadership Refocused, and offer business coaching focusing on the important aspects of personal and professional development.

Conclusion

Forgiveness is a deeply personal and complex journey, but it can really help us heal and grow. Understanding how forgiveness works, recognizing the signs of true forgiveness, and using some practical steps, can help us start this journey with courage and compassion.

Remember, forgiving is not for the other person, it doesn't mean forgetting or saying what happened was okay; it means letting go of bitterness and taking back our power to live happily now. By acknowledging our pain, practicing empathy and understanding, and letting go of resentment, we can find peace and healing.

Looking back to this experience, it was the start of a deep and personal transformation. The power of self-love and forgiveness shines from within and others will see and experience it. At this age, I find myself more beautiful than I was in my twenties and thirties.

May you find peace and strength through your own journey and moving forward.

W Katherine Waite-Gracie

Published Author

https://www.linkedin.com/feed/
https://www.facebook.com/
https://www.instagram.com/katsmyth/
https://mugsandsaucers.gr8.com/

Katherine is a single, homeschooling mom of two great kids. Recently, a best selling author of her first published book, The Mugs & Saucers Cafe, Katherine has been writing poetry and short stories her whole life. Enjoying the creative outlet writing and art have given her through life's ups and downs. Growing her essential oil business, attaining degrees and certificates in Reiki, Canine Specialist, and Children's Yoga, she is kept busy learning alongside her son and daughter as they enjoy the benefits of unschooling together. Growing up in a small town, being part of a community, Katherine hopes to branch out on her own again, supporting herself and her kids, once again becoming part of a community. With hope and faith as her foundation, and consistency and positive manifestation, Katherine's dreams are already coming true.

W! Wilhemina

By W Katherine Waite-Gracie

Hi. I'm Wanda Katherine. I was named after 4 people. No really. Two grammas and two aunts. One of each on my mom's and dad's side. I'm also Kathy, Katherine, Kat, Kate Waite, and Kit Kat. Also known as Saskatoon Berry, Sassafras, Sass, and Sassy. I have been named or tried out one of the other forms of my name, so many times, there are many 'Me's'. It's funny to think about what all the people in my life's history have called me or refer to me as. And I love that with each name and each person, there's a story. But who am I? Which 'Me' *is* Me?

It's quite serendipitous and likens to my story to have so many names. I've always been in search of my true identity. My name often made me uncomfortable because I go by my second name but would get called Wanda, and that name never made me feel "cool." Silly yes, but you know kids. Most of us were one, once, a silly kid of course. If anyone asked what the "W" stood for, I would make a joke about it and say Wilhemina. Pretty sure anyone my age or older might actually have been transported back to Sesame Street reading that name. "W! Wilhemina!" and that's where I got it from. So, I wouldn't tell them it stood for Wanda because Wilhemina was much better than my actual name? *Ya, okay, Kath*! Oh, and there's another name I go by, that I forgot to mention. "Kath." It gets hard to keep track. Well, I soon grew to love my W and what it stood for wholeheartedly, and now more than ever I'm so grateful to have my grandmother's name.

So, back to the serendipity. I use that word because I have worn many hats and played whatever role was required of me at any given moment. I am a kick-ass gopher and am always ready, willing, and at your service. Tell me what to do, and I'll do it! Even if it hurts or drains me. Actually, often, you don't even have to tell me what to do, I'm already conscious of what is needed and jump into fight or flight mode, ready to fill the need. I am happy to help, but my journey is trying very hard to tell me it does not and should not come at the expense of my own health or happiness. Okay W, so, then what? Oh, oh, now who am I? If I'm not ready to report for orders and carry everyone's, as well as my own, loads, then what hat should I be wearing? Wait, I'll just wear my old hats. Maybe they're not comfortable but I know those hats and I've worn them in, really well! Better the devil you know, right? Never really liked that saying, but hey, if the hat fits! Back to the Me I'm working on. As the current, evolving, and aware Me, I try to be conscious of what I say and think, finding ways to turn anything into a positive. I have always seen the good in things and can acknowledge that I am a light barrier wishing to spread love and light to all those around me. I believe very much that what we say and what we think comes to be. Over and over in my life, through struggles and pain, joy and miracles, I have seen what we say and believe come true. Actually, it was the third night of a manifestation journaling entry in June 2023 that brought the first line of my first published book into being, and so far, I haven't stopped writing, every day since that night. I always used to write and draw. I would spend hours writing poetry or journaling in my many diaries. Sketch after sketch, word after word, poem after poem, I found the power of my pencil to be an incredible outlet. Somewhere along the way, I stopped though. Life got busier, more complicated and I realize now, I became less of a friend to myself and closed myself up, retreating more deeply into the shell this Cancerian sign is known to do. Not doing anything for myself or any kind of healing or growth, and once again, I suddenly didn't exist. My corner was darker than ever. I was fortunate to admit this to an old friend and she was the one who suggested the manifestation journal. I will forever be grateful for that idea and the floodgate it has opened within me. I have 1 published book, 2 more complete and ready to be released later this year, 5 more in the works, and now here I am, writing in this awesome Anthology.

I'm so proud to be part of this amazing women's movement of voices. Pretty wonderful what a sickly, almost paralyzed, and blind little girl, living in alcoholism, now single momma of two, homeschooling and falling forward through life with my essential oils in hand woman, had to sludge through to find the glimmers and life lessons. I have kept so much of myself hidden, literally and figuratively, always searching for the Me that will fit in, unnoticed, or minimally noticed, and hopefully doing anything and everything the right way, and without causing any trouble or being in any way, shape, or form the reason trouble might incur. Oh ya, make sure all other parties around me are following the same guideline, and not setting off any time bombs either. And don't forget to smile! Hey, wait, let's add getting sicker, and sicker. How about deathly sick, which leads me to my first life miracle. One more week without removing the tumor would have been the reason for paralysis and blindness. I was told about the "almost" at a follow-up appointment a year after my close to 6-hour brain surgery. Un-treated? Well… My story would have been a lot shorter. I'm 45 and I am still healing from the trauma of that sickness, surgery, and recovery. Sure, I've healed physically and in many ways emotionally as well. But the physical part still has its repercussions. Scar tissue can cause issues as well, as it heals and changes, sometimes other health problems develop, and although I am much better off than that sick little girl was or could have been, there have been some health hurdles along the way, creating other roadblocks, giving space for old trauma to visit again, but luckily, also offering room for healing and growth. I wrote my first book when I was 13. It was about a little girl who was dying. My brain surgery was the day before my 13th birthday and it became my second birthday, which I still celebrate every year. In writing that first book, it was another one of those unimaginable, horrific parts of life that I have been blessed to overcome and learn from. Writing my story about what I had gone through was a huge healing experience. Although it was fictional, it was based on *my* story. While I wrote, sitting on the floor in the back corner of the school library during lunch, my friends would gather around me, reading it, asking me questions, making suggestions, and asking if they could be in it too! Some people wanted to see the 10-inch scar running down the back of my head and neck, asking questions about what it was like. My shaved hair grew back quickly and the 1 ½ disks in my neck they filed down and removed to get where they needed to, adding to the "WOW" moments of question time. As I type these words I feel uneasy, and the tunnel vision that comes before passing out rises like a tidal wave, rolling up behind me in an attempt to consume me… Deep breath in… Long slow breath out… Breathe in the light… Exhale the darkness. Back to the gathered friends and my first book. As I cast my thoughts back to those moments, and as I write about it now, I'm filled with such love and acceptance. What a beautiful blessing to come out of, from such an ugly, scary, painful chapter in my young life. "It's not about the destination, but the journey." A friend taught me that when I was 20, and I think about it frequently. I've recently heard an add-on, "and who you journey with." And that makes my heart smile as I think about how lucky I have been with the people I have been blessed to know and love. As I grow older, the easier it is to see what I want in my life, or maybe more realistically, what I don't want in my life. The situations, the work, the places, the people, my time, my health. Everything becomes a little clearer along the way.

Although I'm still not sure which Me is Me, I'm loving all of them more than I used to. I know I want to be seen and heard. I want to exist where I belong and build the life my kids and I want to have together. Feeling free and safe and calm and happy. I know I have felt pride in myself that I never felt before, in my recent authoring journey, and knowing how proud my kids are as they watch me stumble along, picking myself up and dusting myself off, soaring and glowing, and all the ups and downs have filled me with such gratefulness and motivation. These are my "WHYS."

I grew up with a strong faith. I went to church every Sunday, followed the love of Jesus, and treated others with love and compassion. I am still walking in faith. I am also more spiritual and more open to the powers of this universe and all its wonders. There are so many things we don't understand and won't ever learn. I wish we had more time to grow here on this beautiful planet. There is a quote from the book *The Big Leap* by Gay Hendricks that I have been saying for over a year now. "I expand in abundance, success and love, every day, as I inspire those around me to do the same." It started off as a mantra that I liked. It has become a testament to the beauty and opportunities blooming all around me. I am a lover of all living things, and I am so blessed to be able to spread love in ways I could never have imagined. Writing has brought love to me through so many facets and outcomes. The joy and fulfillment, healing and growth are beyond words. I am thankful every day for my foundation in faith. I have added daily gratitude and manifestation practice to my daily prayers. If I could tell 13-year-old me what 45-year-old me would be doing, I would have believed in myself a lot sooner. But then, would I still be "this me?" We are all faced with challenges, but we must never give up. Some days, weeks, months, even years seem to be hopeless. I have faced so many closed doors feeling defeated, forgetting that everything happens for a reason and exactly when it's supposed to. Likewise, all the things we thought should happen that didn't, were for good reasons too. Keep going. Never stop. Even when you move forward one step and go back two, keep moving forward. Take the leaps. Do the hard things. Focus on the goal, as unattainable as it might seem, and you will one day arrive at a place that tells you that you are on the right path. Enjoy all the joy and sorrow, for it all holds glimmers and treasured lessons if we shift our outlook. That brings me back to the serendipity and power of our thoughts and words. Living hidden in my crab shell, I never really wanted the limelight to cast its glow upon me. Not too brightly. I have always been great at hiding in the corner, not making waves and being and doing exactly what was expected of me and jumping in, to still the waters around me, then shrinking back to my shell or corner. I have struggled with ailments my whole life. Going to countless doctor's appointments trying to figure out what was wrong with me, to no avail. I tried tinted glasses in the hopes it was the fluorescent lights at school that were causing my daily headaches. I went to a psychologist who declared, "It's just a faze. Probably puberty. She'll grow out of it." Tried different diets in case it was a food allergy or gave up certain treats and gum that had smells that triggered headaches, and the list went on. Still, years later, I didn't know what was wrong, and things were getting worse. I have memories of countless nights falling asleep, playing out a scenario of myself lying in a hospital bed, dying. It was all very Anne of Green Gables and desperately romantic, but I believed I would die from a terrible illness. Imagining people coming and crying at my side, praying for my miraculous recovery, my crushes professing their love for me, and saying goodbye to those I loved. At twelve, I read a book called *13 Is Too Young To Die* and found so many similarities to the main characters' health issues that it was eerie. The character died at the end of that book, and I thought it was a sign for sure. My headaches grew more intense, never stopping, turning into migraines. My bedroom calendar was covered in black X's on the days I had marked off as days with a headache, of which there were many. I began blacking out whenever I lifted my arms, dropping to the floor or being caught by the one holding me if it happened during a hug. Still unaware of the masses growing inside my brain and being pressed upon, with that particular movement, and causing the blackout of my own weakening body. My sight was going, slowly, day by day, I saw less and less. It was like a sheet of black paper was constantly held in front of the top half of my eyes. I was nauseous and dizzy and fading away. The day before my 13th birthday, the tumor and cyst were removed and I spent 2 weeks in Sick Kids Hospital healing, doing daily physio to learn to walk again. I dropped down to half my weight and ate very little, lying in my hospital bed surrounded by loved ones. Somehow, I think I had something to do with how it all ended up. In my deep need to be seen and heard, my body held so much sadness and longing and I had no tools to process it all. Our bodies are beautiful machines that listen and cope, and mine stored so much of it all, that it grew sick, and although I didn't want to be sick anymore, I was finally seen.

In recent years, I have been working on using my thoughts and words to manifest the life I dream of. It has not been easy, and I am not where I want to be…yet! But I recognize that I'm on my way. As I let go and let God, open my heart to the power of the universe, release old trauma and pain, and open myself up to positive possibilities embracing the second chance at life I was gifted, I am finally seeing beautiful things blossoming all around me again. Doors are finally opening. I am in the midst of becoming ME. W K Waite-Gracie. That's me, and my voice is growing stronger, my heart is filling and overflowing, and my light is shining through the cracks in my shelled armor. I am The Girl In The Corner No More, and I will never wear that hat again. I feel like this statement will be one of my personal tests, which I must continue to overcome and grow through, but it is a statement I desire to embrace wholeheartedly.

Whatever you call me, W, Wilhemina, Katherine, Kathy, Kat, Kate Waite, Saskatoon Berry, Sassafras, Sassy, Sass, or Kath, I am ME. And for the first time in my life, I think I'll let my hair blow free and leave my hats hanging on their hooks. As I spread my arms wide, my heart open to many wonders, and raise my wings high, I leave my corner and become the loving, shining, beautiful Me I have always been searching for. Do you hear me? Do you see me? Here I am. I am ME! I am strong and ready to live. Look out world, here I come!

Tracey Booker

Agape Ink LLC
Chief Visionary Officer and Founder

https://www.linkedin.com/in/traceybooker1/
https://www.facebook.com/tracey.booker.92
https://www.instagram.com/angelfor1978
https://agapeink.com/

Tracey Booker is a devoted mother and intuitive writer from Detroit, Michigan, known for her powerful book series In the Quest for Love. Her work explores the emotional and psychological complexities of healing from trauma, particularly focusing on domestic violence and abuse. Through her heartfelt narratives, Tracey highlights the hidden struggles of victims, emphasizing the importance of self-worth, healing, and resilience.

Her personal journey of overcoming adversity deeply informs her writing, blending themes of spiritual growth and personal transformation. In her second volume, Illusions of Loyalty, Tracey reveals how misplaced loyalty can trap individuals in harmful cycles while offering a path to hope and recovery.

With a mission to inspire change and foster understanding, Tracey's work resonates with readers from all walks of life. Her inclusive approach welcomes everyone, regardless of belief system, empowering them to reclaim their voices and embrace a journey of healing. Visit Agapeink.com to learn more.

High Octane Empowerment

By Tracey Booker

Introduction

Tawny was a spirited soul who loved adventure and cherished her vintage car deeply. She understood the importance of giving her vehicle the best care possible, from regular maintenance to using the highest-quality fuel. She believed her car deserved nothing less because it took her on incredible journeys.

One day, Tawny planned a road trip to the mountains. At the gas station, she faced a choice: a promotional deal on lower octane fuel caught her eye. Tempted by the cheaper price, she hesitated but thought, "Maybe just this once."

As Tawny ventured into the mountains, her car began to struggle. It made strange noises and lost power, and she felt a sinking regret. Consulting her manual, she realized she had used the wrong fuel. After correcting her mistake, her car gradually regained its vigor.

Reflecting on her journey, Tawny realized a profound truth: just as her car needed the right fuel to thrive, so did she. She saw the importance of giving herself the best care and support in life's journey. Tawny learned to honor her needs and resilience when facing challenges or setbacks.

This story resonates deeply with women worldwide. It reminds us that we are resilient, capable, and deserving of the best care, like Tawny's vintage car. Just as Tawny's car flourished with proper fuel, so do we when we make choices that honor our well-being. Remember to fuel ourselves with self-compassion, seek the appropriate support, and nurture our inner strength. Together, we can journey through life's ups and downs with resilience and grace.

A woman with a voice is, by definition, a strong woman.

The term "glass ceiling" first appeared in the late 20th century, describing women's invisible barriers to reaching the highest levels of leadership and professional success. These barriers often stem from systemic sexism, gender biases, and cultural norms. Despite these challenges, countless women have broken through these barriers and paved the way for future generations.

Unleashing the Power Within in the heart of Detroit, MI, amidst the hustle and bustle of urban life, a group of women gathered in a nondescript building, drawn together by a shared desire for something more. Among them was Tawny, a young woman whose journey had been marked by resilience, determination, and an unwavering belief in her potential.

Tawny's story begins in a rough neighborhood in the inner city, where she faced adversity from a young age—raised by a single mother who suffered from domestic violence and mental illness. Tawny learned the value of hard work and perseverance early on. Tawny was determined to excel despite her challenges.

But behind Tawny's outward success lay a hidden struggle—a battle with trauma and self-doubt that threatened to overshadow her accomplishments. From a young age, Tawny had experienced witnessing abuse, leaving deep emotional scars that lingered into adulthood. Despite her best efforts to bury the pain, it continued to haunt her, manifesting in anxiety, depression, and a sense of unworthiness.

It wasn't until Tawny crossed paths with Deborah, a seasoned entrepreneur with a passion for empowering women, that she began to see a glimmer of hope. Deb had built her successful business from the ground up, overcoming obstacles and setbacks with grace and resilience. Inspired by Deb's strength and determination, Tawny believed she could rise above her circumstances and create a better life for herself and her family.

Together, Tawny and Deborah embarked on a journey of self-discovery and empowerment, forming the foundation of what would become the High-Octane Empowerment program. Through intensive workshops, seminars, and group therapy sessions, they guided women on a path of healing and transformation, helping them to confront their past traumas and reclaim their power.

For Tawny, the journey was both challenging and cathartic. As she delved deep into her pain and struggles, she began to unravel the layers of fear and self-doubt that had held her back for so long. With the support of her fellow sisters in empowerment, Tawny learned to release the emotional baggage weighing her down, freeing herself to step into her full potential.

Cultivating Financial Independence

As Tawny and her fellow empowerment sisters delved deeper into their journey of self-discovery, they turned their attention to finances—a domain often fraught with uncertainty and insecurity, especially for women. Guided by Deb's expertise in entrepreneurship and financial literacy, they embarked on a quest to build financial independence and stability.

For Tawny, who had grown up in a household where money was always tight, financial freedom seemed like an impossible dream. But with Sarah's guidance and support, she began to see new possibilities opening up before her. Together, they explored budgeting, investing, and entrepreneurship, empowering women to take control of their financial futures.

As Tawny immersed herself in finance, she discovered a newfound sense of confidence and empowerment. No longer content to survive paycheck to paycheck, she set her sights on building wealth and creating a legacy for herself and her family. With Deb's mentorship, Tawny launched her own business—a small but thriving enterprise that provided financial security and stability for herself and those she loved.

But empowerment wasn't just about accumulating wealth—it was about using it to uplift and empower others. Inspired by Sarah's example, Maya advocated for financial literacy and empowerment, sharing her knowledge and expertise with women in her community. Through workshops, seminars, and one-on-one coaching sessions, she helped women overcome their fears and insecurities around money, empowering them to take control of their financial destinies.

Rising Together

As Tawny and her fellow empowerment sisters continued their journey of self-discovery and empowerment, they began to realize the true power of sisterhood. **A woman's strength** comes from lifting each other and standing together in solidarity. United by a common purpose and a shared vision for a better future, they forged bonds of friendship and sisterhood that would withstand the test of time.

Together, they confronted the challenges and obstacles that stood in their way, drawing strength from each other's courage and resilience. When one sister stumbled, the others offered support and encouragement, reminding her of her inner strength and resilience. And when one sister succeeded, the others rejoiced, celebrating her victories as if they were their own.

Through their collective efforts, Tawny and her fellow empowerment sisters began to create real and lasting change in their lives and their communities. They volunteered at local shelters, organized fundraising events, and spoke out against injustice, using their voices and resources to uplift and empower those in need. As they continued to rise, they inspired others to do the same, igniting a ripple effect of positive change that spread far beyond their circle.

In the end, Tawny and her fellow empowerment sisters stood tall, their hearts ablaze with the fire of empowerment, their spirits fueled by the limitless potential within each one of them. They had not only raised their vibrations but had become beacons of hope and inspiration for women everywhere, proving that when women come together, there is no obstacle too significant, no dream too ambitious, and no goal beyond reach. For in the sisterhood of empowerment, anything is possible.

Triumph of the Spirit. In the end.

Tawny's persistence and resilience led her to triumph. She emerged from the ashes of her past, a beacon of hope for others who walked a similar path. She empowered those around her with the wisdom gained from her struggles, spreading light and love wherever she went. As the story of Tawny's journey ended, a chorus of voices rose to celebrate her triumph. She was not just a survivor but a warrior whose courage and strength inspired a generation of women to rise above their circumstances and embrace their true potential. The essence of a woman overcoming trauma, gaining financial literacy, bravery, and the power of faith while maintaining a light-heartedness and a great sense of humor propelled to a higher level of consciousness. Tawny's pride and joy have been part of building her brand, Agapeink.com. Once you reach a level in life and overcome struggles, your badge of honor is that you have grown your extra layer of skin to continue the good fight. Tawny's vision to meet a large audience of listeners and readers was pulled from her admiration of one of the greats, Maya Angelo. Tawny discovered herself after encountering a powerful poem by the late Maya Angelou.

"You may write me down in history with your bitter, twisted lies; you may trod me in the very dirt, but still, like dust, I'll rise. Does my sassiness upset you? Why are you beset with gloom? 'Cause I walk like I've got oil wells pumping in my living room. Just like moons and like suns, With the certainty of tides, just like hopes springing high, Still I'll rise. Did you want to see me broken? Bowed head and lowered eyes? Shoulders falling down like tear drops. Weakened by my soulful cries. Does my haughtiness offend you? Don't take it awful hard Cause I laugh like I've got gold mines digging in my own backyard. You may shoot me with your words, you may cut me with your eyes, you may kill me with your hatefulness, but still, like air, I'll rise. Does my sexiness upset you? Does it come as a surprise that I dance like I've got diamonds at the meeting of my thighs? Out of the huts of history's shame, I rise up from a past that's rooted in pain. I rise I'm a black ocean, leaping and wide, welling and swelling; I bear in the tide. Leaving behind nights of terror and fear, I rise into a daybreak that's wondrously clear. I rise, bringing the gifts that my ancestors gave; I am the dream and the hope of the slave. I rise, I rise, I rise." - Maya Angelo.

Reasoning with Your Pain: A Journey to Healing and Understanding the Weight of Pain

Tawny, a woman in her early thirties, found herself drowning in an ocean of grief. Her eldest sister and mother had passed away suddenly, leaving her alone to raise their young daughter. The sorrow was relentless, and every corner of their home echoed memories of happier times. Tawny felt trapped in a cycle of pain and despair, unable to find a way out. One day, while sifting through some old books, Tawny came across a journal her husband had kept. Inside, she found a note he had written, urging her to "reason with her pain" if she ever felt overwhelmed. Though she didn't fully understand what he meant, the words resonated deeply. Desperate for relief, Tawny decided to embark on a journey to make sense of her grief and find a path to healing.

Seeking guidance, Tawny sought a renowned therapist known for her empathetic approach to trauma and loss. Tawny poured out her heart to her therapist, describing the weight of her grief and the note from her husband. "Reasoning with your pain means understanding it, acknowledging it, and finding a way to live with it. It's not about eliminating the pain but transforming your relationship with it. Explore Tawny's grief and understand its origins; one visit with the therapist is not the remedy; yes, you may feel some reprieve and less pressure; however, more work is needed to break through to get you on the path to your life purpose. Develop strategies to cope with it. Tawny agreed, feeling a glimmer of hope for the first time since her husband's death. Exploration during their sessions, her therapist guided Tawny through three key phases: acknowledging pain, understanding its roots, and finding constructive ways to cope.

Acknowledging Pain: Dr. Carter encouraged Tawny to confront her grief head-on rather than suppressing it. She asked Tawny to write letters to her late husband, expressing her sorrow, anger, and love. These letters became a cathartic outlet for Tawny, allowing her to articulate emotions she had been too afraid to face. Understanding Its Roots: Through deep conversations and reflective exercises, Tawny began to uncover the layers of her pain. She realized that her grief was not only about losing her husband but also about the future they had planned together and the fear of raising their daughter alone. Understanding these layers helped Tawny see her pain more clearly and compassionately. Finding Constructive Ways to Cope: Dr. Carter introduced various coping mechanisms, such as mindfulness, journaling, and creating new routines. Tawny started practicing daily routines, making new memories while honoring the past. The support group became a second family, providing a network of understanding and encouragement.

The Ripple Effect

Tawny's journey of reasoning with her pain inspired those around her. Her friends and family, witnessing her transformation, began to address their struggles with loss and trauma. Tawny shared the tools and insights she had gained, helping others to confront and understand their pain. Motivated by her progress, Tawny started a blog called Reasoning with Pain, where she documented her journey and offered advice to others facing similar challenges. The blog quickly gained a following, becoming a source of hope and guidance for many.

A Legacy of Healing

Years later, Tawny stood before a group at a community center, leading a workshop titled "Reasoning with Your Pain." She looked out at people's faces, eager to find solace and understanding, just as she had once been. With a heart full of empathy and strength, Tawny began her talk, "Welcome, everyone. Today, we journey to understand our pain, reason with it, and ultimately find healing." As she spoke, Tawny knew that her husband's words had led her to a place of profound transformation. The legacy of healing and understanding she had built was a testament to the power of confronting and reasoning with pain, turning it into a source of strength and resilience.

Tawny wants you to Level Up Your Purpose by Fueling Women's Rise to Mental, Financial, and Emotional Stability, the transformative journey to achieve mental, financial, and emotional stability. Men and women from various backgrounds are struggling with the demands of life. Behind the eyes of the pain and a mix of hope and skepticism, wondering if things will begin to shift once you find your purpose to reclaim your power, redefine your goals, and rise to new heights. We're here to level up our purpose before we leave this planet. So, overcoming adversity and transforming from a struggling single mother to a successful entrepreneur and mentor, Tawny's journey was inspiring and set the tone for this message: the sooner you realize that you are on borrowed time, you will be less likely to hold on to old wounds, that cannot grow you. It takes up space that can be used for a more positive purpose of forward movement toward the path you are meant to be on. Three key grounded elements are mental stability, financial empowerment, and emotional resilience. Each segment provides practical tools and strategies to help individuals overcome their challenges. Mental strength, mindfulness, and the power of positive thinking, as well as emphasizing self-care, setting boundaries, and seeking professional help. Go within and reflect on your mental health... Financial Empowerment: Break down complex concepts into manageable steps to make budgeting, saving, and investing manageable. Learn the importance of financial literacy and small, consistent steps toward financial freedom—emotional resilience, emotional intelligence, self-awareness, and building a supportive community. The stories of other women, the practical advice, and the collective energy can and will be very beneficial and healing.

Understanding who you are and what works best for you is critical—leveling up your purpose to create harmony and fulfillment. Attend therapy sessions, create a budget, and join a support group. Set new career goals, pursuing further education and skill development. The Ripple Effect: now that you have awakened to a high self, indirectly, you have inspired other women to seek their paths to stability and empowerment. Tawny started a blog to share her experiences and tips, reaching women beyond her immediate circle. She became a mentor, partnering with Deb to organize workshops and support groups. Together, they helped countless women fulfill their purpose, fostering mental, financial, and emotional stability.

The Legacy

Years later, Tawny stood on the same stage where her journey began, now a co-speaker at the "Level Up Your Purpose" seminar. She looked at the eager faces, women ready to embark on their transformative journeys. With gratitude and purpose, Tawny began her speech, "Welcome, ladies. Today, we journeyed to reclaim our power, redefine our goals, and rise to new heights. Together, we will level up our purpose." The legacy of empowerment continued one woman at a time, creating a world where mental, financial, and emotional stability were not just dreams but achievable realities.

Let's unpack a few powerful prayers. Tawny encourages individuals to meditate on Psalm 91 a powerful scripture in the Bible that speaks of God's protection and deliverance. Here is the full text of Psalm 91 from the New International Version (NIV): 1." Pslams 91" Whoever dwells in the shelter of the Most High will rest in the shadow of the Almighty. 2. I will say of the Lord, "He is my refuge and my fortress, my God, in whom I trust." 3. Surely, he will save you from the Fowler's snare and from the deadly pestilence. 4. He will cover you with his feathers, and under his wings, you will find refuge; his faithfulness will be your shield and rampart. 5. You will not fear the terror of night, nor the arrow that flies by day, 6. nor the pestilence that stalks in the darkness, nor the plague that destroys at midday. 7. A thousand may fall at your side, ten thousand at your right hand, but it will not come near you. 8. You will only observe with your eyes and see the punishment of the wicked. 9. If you say, "The Lord is my refuge," and you make the Most High your dwelling, 10. no harm will overtake you; no disaster will come near your tent. 11. For he will command his angels concerning you to guard you in all your ways; 12. They will lift you up in their hands so that you will not strike your foot against a stone. 13. You will tread on the lion and the cobra; you will trample the great lion and the serpent. 14. "Because he loves me," says the Lord, "I will rescue him; I will protect him, for he acknowledges my name. 15. He will call on me, and I will answer him; I will be with him in trouble, I will deliver him and honor him. 16. With long life, I will satisfy him and show him my salvation."

"Psalm 23 is one of the Bible's most well-known and cherished Psalms. It is a Psalm of David and speaks of God's guidance, provision, and comfort. Here is the full text of Psalm 23 from the New International Version (NIV): Psalm 23 1. The Lord is my shepherd; I lack nothing. 2. He makes me lie down in green pastures, he leads me beside quiet waters; 3. he refreshes my soul. He guides me along the right paths for his name's sake. 4. Even though I walk through the darkest valley, I will fear no evil, for you are with me; your rod and your staff, they comfort me. 5. You prepare a table before me in the presence of my enemies. You anoint my head with oil; my cup overflows. 6. Surely your goodness and love will follow me all the days of my life, and I will dwell in the house of the Lord forever."

Reflection

In the winding roads of life, we often find ourselves navigating through challenges and uncertainties, much like Tawny and her vintage car journeying into the mountains. Tawny's story serves as a poignant reminder of the importance of giving ourselves the best care possible, akin to providing the proper fuel for a cherished vehicle. Just as Tawny learned that her car thrived with adequate octane, we also thrive when prioritizing our well-being and resilience.

As women worldwide, we often wear many hats—caregivers, professionals, nurturers, and dreamers. Amid our busy lives, it's easy to overlook our needs or settle for less than what we truly deserve. Tawny's moment of reflection invites us to pause and consider: Are we giving ourselves the best care and support in our journeys?

Self-care isn't selfish; it's essential. It's about recognizing our worth and nurturing our physical, emotional, and spiritual health. Just as Tawny's car required regular maintenance and the right fuel to perform optimally, so do we need to invest in ourselves. This investment isn't just for our benefit but also for those around us, our families, communities, and society. When prioritizing our well-being, we become better equipped to handle life's challenges and support others effectively.

Moreover, Tawny's experience teaches us about resilience. Life inevitably presents us with obstacles and moments when we feel like we're running on the wrong fuel, struggling to find our strength. Yet, like Tawny correcting her course and restoring her car's performance, we, too, can bounce back from setbacks. Resilience isn't about avoiding difficulties but embracing them with courage and learning from them. It's about trusting in our ability to adapt and grow stronger, no matter what life throws our way.

Each of us has a unique journey filled with triumphs, trials, and unexpected detours. In these moments, our resilience shines brightest when we draw upon our inner resources, seek support from others, and navigate through adversity with grace and determination. Tawny's story reminds us that resilience isn't just a trait; it's a skill we can cultivate through self-awareness, self-compassion, and a willingness to learn and evolve.

We connect as women through our shared experiences of striving, overcoming, and thriving. Tawny's journey resonates with us because it reflects our pursuit of balance, fulfillment, and purpose. Whether in the driver's seat or navigating uncharted paths, let us remember the power of self-care and resilience.

Let us commit to honoring our needs, embracing our strengths, and supporting each other in our collective journey toward growth and fulfillment. Together, we can create a world where every woman feels empowered to prioritize her well-being, pursue her dreams, and contribute meaningfully to her communities.

In closing, let Tawny's story inspire us to fuel ourselves with self-compassion, resilience, and a steadfast belief in our inherent worth. May we continue to journey forward with courage, compassion, and a deep appreciation for the journey.

Krista Sobieski

Founder of Thoughtful Seed Project

https://www.linkedin.com/in/krista-sobieski-12608326
https://www.facebook.com/kjsobieski
https://unimaginablehope.org/

Krista Sobieski is the founder of the Thoughtful Seed Project of Central Wisconsin. A farmer's wife and mother of four who has a strong background in early education, leadership development, and community collaborations and loves to write and share her voice. She writes about topics including life, death, parenting, fundraising, motivation, and teamwork, just to name a few. Krista lives in the country, believes in the greater God, and has worked in an early childhood setting for 23 years. She is the founder of Unimaginable Hope, a non-

profit charity with a mission to spread kindness and bring hope to those who need it. In a moment of darkness, Unimaginable Hope was created in memory of her parents, whom she lost on the same day.

Authentic Love Starts from Your Own Heart

By Krista Sobieski

Life is interesting, and I firmly believe that the stories in our lives capture the moments and memories that help shape us, inspire us, and form us. Everyone has a story, and everyone has a story to tell. Some stories are funny, some are sad, some are inspiring, and some stories are unbelievable. Regardless, if we realize it, our own stories and those of others impact our lives.

I have a story, and although I don't always share it all, I hope the parts I have shared and continue to share have or will inspire someone else, have or will help someone else or maybe even make them laugh, and at times, even force them to look at life and the space around them differently.

Stories are meant to be told, and there is nothing better than a good story. A book, an article, or even a simple note can share a story. Even if it has taken me some time to figure out a lot of things and life, and though I am still learning, once you hit a certain time in life, you will start to let go of what holds you back and just live. It's a work in progress to do this, and I am learning that. Sharing this, sometimes, is the first step of letting go and being authentic. Being part of *100 Voices of Women* is an honor as it's one time I can really use my voice to share and be heard. At times, life can seem so discouraging, yet to me, it's simple.

Sharing my personal stories and those of others does matter. It's the stories of ordinary and extraordinary people, places, and things that make us think, laugh, and cry. Stories can change lives and can give hope, stories can make us see the sun on a cloudy day, make us feel deep in our souls, and even ignite a spark to start a fire that burns deep inside of us to live fully content. Stories impact us all in different ways.

What's my hope? My hope is that when I write, I bring a more positive vibe to this life and help inspire others. For me, this is a step in planting my own seed, with fulfilling my dream of becoming a published author. I have done that with my first published book, *Giving into Hope*, which was released in the Spring of 2024, and now I am part of this incredible book, too! A great writing mentor once told me that the only way you become a good writer logically, is to take the first step and "just write and write a little every day!" So, today I write for this wonderful anthology, and I hope to give others the great insight that I wish I had as my younger self.

While I can't promise what I write will resonate with everyone, it will be realistic. I hope it provides thoughts that provoke you, gives you little tidbits of everything in this world that amazes me, and plants thoughts in your head that will encourage you!

In 2016, I found out that I was being targeted in a business matter gone wrong, in 2017, both of my parents passed on the same day, and from 2020 to 2023, I worked under a leader who was toxic, a habitual liar, and made me feel about as bad about myself as anyone could.

Can you imagine being a successful businessperson, feeling like you are making a difference in the world, and being recognized for your work and commitment to those you serve? Then, suddenly go from being confident, strong-willed, and dedicated to feeling depressed, insecure, and trying to balance life so that you still raise healthy, well-rounded kids.

From 2016 to 2023, my life took a downward spiral, and even though I put on a happy face and found a way to care and love those around me, I had a hard time loving myself and felt ashamed, tired, and very anxious.

It is so easy to succumb to social pressure, lose your true self, and get lost in a world that is filled with expectations and judgment. It is so hard to be authentically yourself in fear of judgment and not feeling normal. Let me tell you, it's important to be true to yourself and find ways to align your life with your values, embrace your potential, self-acceptance, and much more to live an authentic lifestyle.

It's okay for you to become the champion of your own life and explore what can happen when you let down your guard to really dive deep into your own interest and allow others to really see who you are. Embrace your unique, personal self, make it okay to live by your core values, and walk away from people and things that don't align. Understand that not everyone will love you and like you but stand tall anyway and know we were not expected to be friends with everyone. Listen to what's inside you. Figure out how to listen to your inner voice, challenge societal norms, nurture your mental health and well-being, and make choices that prioritize your true authenticity.

The truth is you sacrifice so much, and every time, you sacrifice yourself at the altar of societal norms and conformity. Like me, if you continue to do that, you will lack happiness and a sense of fulfillment in life. When you are not true to yourself, you may experience the following things like I did. I struggled with anxiety, depression, not eating right, and worse yet, you may face addiction or rage. I was grateful that most of my issues were emotional, and I could still self-regulate enough to keep on top of myself even though it was hard.

I learned to self-reflect and that helped a lot! A big step forward in living authentically is reflecting on your life and looking into areas that are not aligned with who you are. Take time to understand yourself, your strengths, weaknesses, passions, and values. Reflect on your past experiences and how they have shaped you.

All the situations I had been through in a short time hurt and controlled me. I sought help. I went to counseling. It took six years. Don't wait; if you need help, ask for it. Being a writer, I learned that a good way to reflect is to have a journal and write, and then go back and read. This helps you understand and relook at your feelings and ideas.

It helps you see your reactions and think about why you reacted in a certain way. It helps you better understand moments and how you reacted.

When you are authentic and true to yourself, you start to trust your inner wisdom and intuition to guide you in making decisions aligned with your authentic self. Your intuition is a powerful tool that communicates your deepest desires, values, and needs. Practice tuning into your intuition through quiet reflection, meditation, or simply by paying attention to subtle feelings and sensations. Honor the messages your intuition sends, even if they contradict rational thought or societal expectations. Your inner knowing is a powerful guide when we learn to listen and take action. Your intuition is your inner voice pointing to a more authentic life. It's not easy to do, yet why should it be so hard to live happy and healthy? I learned the hard way, trying to be a people pleaser and allowing hurt to creep in. When you feel shame, anxiety, and hurt, it's harder to live true to yourself.

In this chapter, I simply want to share tips on how to live authentically. First, set some boundaries and be a protector of your time and well-being, and see how your energy changes. It's okay to say no, and it takes time to learn this. Learn to say no to things that don't resonate with your values or goals. Do not ignore your own needs. Chances are you have a lot of people depending on you, and if you always put them first, you probably are putting yourself on the back burner, not attending to youself. I personally gained a lot of weight and was not feeling good. Sometimes, this can go too far, especially when we don't create boundaries to protect our peace and time for self-care. Listen to how you feel and draw a line so you create a peaceful time for yourself.

The hardest thing for me was being honest with myself. I was struggling, though I had a hard time admitting it. It's very important to practice self-awareness and honesty.

Don't be afraid to honor your feelings, desires, and fears without judgment. Avoid pretending to be someone you're not or conforming to others' expectations. Acknowledge what you feel and act accordingly, as lying to yourself, you will find that you are unhappy and find yourself in a dark place, stuck or lost.

Don't be afraid to embrace vulnerability because authenticity requires vulnerability. Be open to showing your true self, including your imperfections and insecurities. Vulnerability fosters genuine connections with others.

When you are vulnerable, and you let your guard down to those who are deserving, you develop real relationships and connections with the right people. Real relationships are extremely important. You learn to have self-compassion and learn how to love yourself. I had been beaten down so much, I had so much self-doubt. I had to learn to treat myself better. You have to shower yourself with kindness and compassion. You have to start understanding that authenticity is a journey, and it's okay to make mistakes along the way. We learn from what we love, and you can learn and grow from your experiences and use them to flourish. In many cases, we are so hard on ourselves and struggle to accept ourselves as we are. It's like a voice gets in our heads, and we talk harshly when we fail or make mistakes. We don't reset and move on but get stuck with self-hate and start to feel obligated and overwhelmed as we want others to appreciate us more. We need to be kinder to ourselves. We need to rest, we need to understand it's normal to need support, and we need to accept that it's okay to break down every now and then and have a support system that helps us get back up. Make it okay to enjoy things you like and do things to have fun. Reward yourself and give yourself the grace to do things at your own pace.

It's okay to be proud of yourself and celebrate by enjoying life. I have learned to practice mindfulness and stay in the moment. I pay more attention to how I am feeling and honor what I am feeling. It's important to pay attention to your thoughts and emotions without judgment. Being mindful helps us stay connected to our authentic selves.

We can continue to grow and keep improving while staying true to ourselves if we are willing to keep learning, exploring, and evolving. Just remember to stay grounded in your values and authenticity. Stay open-minded, make it okay to learn from others, and never allow someone to think and speak for you. This is what I had started to do. This is where I lost myself and started to let self-doubt in. Life changes us. Situations change us, yet remember to not let negative things define you.

Remind yourself often that change is okay, and that you will evolve more as you grow.

When you self-love, you will start to gravitate where the love is. You will start to find and build friendships that go both ways and will find those who appreciate you. You will start to find open doors and meaningful communication that is good, honest, and authentic.

When this happens, you will feel an energy shift, and you will be uplifted! Your health and overall wellness will improve, and the intentions within you and around you will be pure.

When we are true to ourselves and allow others to be equally authentic, the spotlight shines on everyone equally. Authenticity is a beautiful gift. You are no longer afraid, and the confidence within you starts to shine. When you value yourself, others will start to value you, too! It really is beautiful when you let go of what you can't change, start to feel unashamed and brave, and take a step back to live exactly how you might like, too. Life is too short to blame yourself for events and situations you cannot control. When you love yourself, you will go where the love is, and you will feel it radiate back.

Through a lot of healing, I have learned to forgive myself—first, for carrying the burdens I didn't deserve to carry—and also to walk a little bit more proud of who I am. Remember that how people treat you has more to do with how they feel about themselves, and when we learn this, we find ways to better regulate and manage our own lives.

Today, I am proud of who I am. I am delighted to be part of this book and share my voice as part of this magnificent group of 100 Women. Share your voice, be heard, and be you! Life is a beautiful gift, and when we share from our own hearts as our true selves, we live as an example. I am a gift, you are a gift, and together we make a difference in this world!

Please consider reading my book, *Giving Into Hope*. I am also the founder of a non-profit, Unimaginable Hope, a charity in memory of my parents, that has a mission to do good in this world. Other anthologies I am part of are *My Unforgettable Personal Journey* and *Her Giving Journey*.

Pamela Kurt

Best Version of You
Coach

https://www.linkedin.com/in/pamela-kurt-41a26ba/
https://www.facebook.com/pam.kurt
https://www.instagram.com/best_version_you/
https://bestversionyou.com
https://pamkurt.com

Pamela D. Kurt is an attorney, best selling author, speaker and life coach. All of the books she has co authored have hit best seller marks in various categories from Women in Business to Self-Help and more.

As an author she has also been featured in various magazines from: Enterprise World; The Fortune Leader; Tycoon Magazine, Exelon Magazine, Becoming an Unstoppable Women, Special Edition, Wealthy Women Entrepreneurs of Influence and contributing author for Brainz Magazine.

But her real passion is Best Version of You, LLC. She empowers women through personal development and spiritual growth. The goal is to empower and elevate women to their next level and be the best version of themselves.

She lives in Ohio with her husband and two black labs. She also enjoys time with her adult son and grandson. You can reach her at pam@bestversionyou.com or https://pamkurt.com

Hear My Voice...

By Pamela Kurt

"Be Still and Know I am God" Psalm 46:10

My name is Pam Kurt. I am sure from the brief introduction of this chapter you learned a little bit about me. I want to share more about me personally. My faith journey started quite young. I grew up in a rural community in Ohio. There were some small farms around, but there were no sidewalks and few streetlights. My grandparents are from Canada and moved to the US when my father was in middle school. They owned a 125-acre farm about 20 miles away that we visited frequently.

I was actually born on an Army military base in Killeen, Texas (my father was in the Army and honorably discharged shortly thereafter my birth due to some medical complications from his surgery while enlisted). He did serve in the US Army (although he came from Canada) during the late 60s and early 70s. Immigration laws, etc., were a lot different back then, especially, during the draft.

My father never finished high school but was very talented and could fix anything. He primarily worked on cars and motors. I grew up (at least as memory serves) very much a "daddy's girl." I would be outside with him a lot! I learned a lot from him ... the basics from swimming, fishing, batting a ball, throwing a frisbee, ice skating, playing billiards, how to catch worms, how to use a knife, how to use basic tools, and more. I look back sometimes and things that I learned as a child, I learned to do left-handed.

My other set of grandparents lived within a few miles from our house. My mother's parents were great and a huge part of my life growing up, too. They were there through the majority of my childhood and adult life. I am ever so grateful for them. Family has always been very important to me and was my foundation.

The reason some history and background about my family and especially my Dad is significant is because my father passed away in a car accident when I was 8 years old. It wasn't an instant car accident. He was hospitalized for over a month before passing away. We didn't get to see him after he had the accident. My mom did bring us to the hospital parking lot once and said my Dad was going to be looking out the window to see us in the parking lot. But I never got to see him again after his accident. As a child, we (my brother and I) only heard updates fit for children. It was weird, and felt like I never got to say goodbye.

The morning of his accident, he left to go to the corner store for tomato soup. My brother and I were left home playing in a plastic tunnel (they used to look like an accordion) while he ran to the store. My mom wasn't home; she was at the hospital visiting my grandmother, who was in the hospital because she had just had surgery. This "corner store" was literally a mile away. He went to get soup because that's what I wanted for lunch. Somehow, when my dad would make the Campbell's soup, it was the best ever. He just literally added a splash of milk and heated it up, but it was the best because he made it.

Later, as I got older and found out or even figured things out, his accident happened before he even got to the store. He was driving a Ford Mustang, the tie rod broke, and the car went off the road and smashed into a telephone pole. He was cut out of the driver's side of the car with the "jaws of life." From the pictures, if you only saw one side of the car, the passenger side wasn't harmed.

My grandfather (we called him papaw) called and asked where my dad was and I told him that he's at the store. See, as I mentioned, I lived in a very small community. The fire department and rescues was already called and they called my grandfather because it looked like my father was in the accident. My grandfather didn't know if it was my dad or not until that call.

As a child, I still didn't really know what was going on, My mom came home and told me and my brother, and my dad stayed in ICU for quite some time. Our house was chaotic, with people coming and going. My mom coming back, kind of telling us kids updates.

Then, one day, I will never forget the image burned into my head. My aunt was over, watching my brother and me, and my cousins were there. At this time, we were all young, so there was some even in high chairs. My grandfather (who was a tall man, over 6 feet and back then seemed even taller to me) came into the house and put his head down. No one said anything to me. I looked up, and all of the women of my family, my grandmother, mom, and Aunt, were all in his arms, crying. I just knew. It was such a sight. All of the women in my family were being held and comforted by my grandfather. I ran to my room; I remember not speaking for days.

My faith background was that I was baptized Lutheran and grew up as a Methodist (the church closest to where we lived). I grew up with my Paternal grandmother (we called her Granny) taking me to church. I was baptized Lutheran and went to Sunday school regularly; I later was confirmed Methodist and baptized my own son Methodist as well. But when I ran to my room at 8 years old, I just started praying and asking why. None of it made sense, and I felt so alone.

I have learnt about religious holidays and stories so much. When my father passed away in April on a Friday, I remember, as a child, thinking he would rise up on Sunday. It was around Easter time. But I also learned fast that religion and faith aren't always the same.

There were many religious things we did for my dad and traditional funeral-type things. But there was such a void and emptiness. Sometimes, I still feel it and yearn for him today. I didn't learn what the faith part even meant until I was older.

This was the first time I questioned God and tried to reconcile faith, religion, and simply why. I would review my life when my dad was in and when he wasn't around. It became a life timeline and marker for the rest of my life. Anything he taught me and I learned before 8 years old is one of my markers. I was left-handed at that time. Later in life, I was taught to become right-handed; so I can print (write) with both hands. I do something as a lefty and most other things with my right hand. So, I have both sides of my brain working at all times. At least, that's how I explain my creativity and logical thinking at the same time. When I was growing up, we didn't have many of the "diagnoses" they have today.

I followed my father in several things, from creative and curious to also struggling with seeing things backwards. I am sure I would fit several other diagnoses, but they didn't diagnose back then. But pretty sure I had some level of dyslexia. My father also had this… of course, from all I learned later in life as an adult and trying to put things together.

My mother later remarried my stepfather, Jim. They are still together today. He was 8 years younger than my mother, but (as my grandmother would say…) bless his heart, my mom gives him a run for it. Later, they had a son, my wonderful stepbrother. So today, I have two brothers whom I love to death!

Throughout my childhood and teenage years, I was a classic overachiever. I had to get good grades and be #1. I played piano, sang in the choir, and tried to be a "good kid." I look back and I was always busy. My busyness to fill the void came quite early. There were times I would go into my room and wonder if anyone cared. I would feel lonely and out of place and would pray to God to show me the way even back then. I started journaling even at a young age and those pages would turn into prayers to God.

I knew and believed that God had never left me. But the pain of feeling sad or empty had stayed with me for a long time.

Another marker in my life was when I turned 18 years old. I had always been the traditional good kid. And I realized at 18 years old, I could leave my mom's house and not come back. So, after a few arguments, that's what I, in fact, did. I stayed at my best friend's parent's house until I graduated (I turned 18 years old in March and still needed to finish high school). Those were dark times. I had scholarship opportunities, college tours, etc. I had no idea what I was doing. I even missed the opportunity for any funding because my father was in the military.

So, at 18 years old, I started working two jobs and attending college, again fulfilling the need to be busy. I didn't know really what to do, but I knew (at least I thought) I was supposed to go to college. I didn't have any financial help, and it was hard. Any guidance on filling out FASFAs, etc., wasn't there. I fumbled through and "made payments" towards any tuition at a local community college. I was trying to start college all on my own. A path of unchartered territory.

I got a job offer in Washington, D.C. I thought if I got here to make some money, I could move to California with my friends. I thought I could go to school cheaper if I moved to California. I never made it to California; I met my ex-husband in D.C. I was alone in D.C., but I wasn't afraid because I was so naïve. God kept me safe in scenarios I didn't even realize were dangerous. I got pregnant, moved back to Ohio, and had my son. We later moved to Miami, Florida, after the baby was born.

At this point, I again started feeling those alone feelings. I started attending church in Miami and even had my son baptized there. When he was baptized, my family never came to visit or to my wedding in D.C. So, somehow, with my father gone, I was simply dismissed. It didn't matter since no one else came either. My marriage wasn't that great, and actually, was quite abusive. I would pray, and I knew God would get me through. There were many days I wanted God to reveal this grand plan. I was very alone inside. But I would literally pray for strength. It worked.

One day after a bad fight, I packed up the crib and came home to Ohio with not much. I literally had to stay at my mom's and grandmother's long enough to work and save up for a car, apartment, etc. Short version, my husband did move back, and we tried (to no avail). Things got worse, and I woke up and literally knew God would take care of me and my son.

I have had many bad times, but I have never doubted that day; God will provide for me. Struggling on and off at one point as a divorced single mom without education, I was let go from my job. I was offered another position thousands of miles away. I elected to be terminated. I heard I could go to school while unemployed. I remember another God moment. I was at the local community college (the one I left years ago). A lady was talking to me and asked where I wanted to be in 5 years. I was giving her reasons why I can't go back and finish school. God put so many right people in place during these years, from scholarships to supportive friendships, and more. Needless to say, I went back to college in the fall, and five years later, I graduated with my associate's, bachelor's, master's, and juris doctorate. I took 20 or more credits a semester and unusually few classes in the summer, but I did it.

God taught me many lessons through those struggling times. One time, I had a stick shift Cavalier for sale. I had gotten another car and wanted to sell the Cavalier. I went and got the title notarized etc., because a lady said she was coming and bringing her daughter to test the car as her first car. I was asking $1500. Well, the daughter didn't want to drive a stick shift, and of course, in my head, I had already spent that money on bills. I was so upset that I even had the title notarized, now what? I was so angry. About a day or so later, another person called for the car. They came. I wasn't excited; still so disappointed. The man came, looked at the car and stated something about "God provides." He was looking for a car he could use to drive back and forth to work. I dismissed it and his words. But then, he offered me $2200 for the car. I knew that God again taking care of me, and I just needed to trust.

Fast forward some more, when I was licensed as an attorney. I was still substitute teaching until I could find a job. I started my own practice and was scared to death, but I was trying to do that and teach to keep an income. I walked into my little law office and remember saying out loud. "God, what am I doing, am I supposed to be a lawyer or a teacher?" I said it out of frustration and fear of not knowing anymore. I asked, and I received…

The next day, I was coming in from teaching when my phone rang. It never stopped. Two people were lined up to come into the law office. What was going on? It exploded. I recruited my son and his teenage friends to help with phones and letters, and I worked late each night. As I grew, God brought the right people and opportunities. There were so many of those kinds of stories. I just needed faith to do as I was to do.

I ended up with over 15 attorneys, 8 support people, and 4 offices. I grew and grew. It was a success—all because I had the faith to do it. I took many business chances and just did it.

I had one attorney (an older man I bought his practice as he retired) say I had more "balls" than most men he knew. I took it as a compliment. But later, while processing, I realized, I didn't even see it as a fear. I knew God was going to get me through.

Time has continued to go forward, and my life has many little times (can be daily, in fact) that God shows me the next steps and comforts me when I am open to hear him. I am on my next journey, and I know I will be taken care of and successful. It's scary to change careers and "start over," but I know God has given me a new direction. I am welcoming this journey. Never give up faith. Life is hard and can be overwhelming. But give that away, God is ready and always there. I know, when you're in the throes of it, it's hard to even see the light at the end of the tunnel or even acknowledge there's a way out. But when we can't see how to get through those storms, let go and have faith— God will get you through.

"My God will supply every need of yours according to his riches in glory in Christ Jesus" (Phil. 4:19).

Carrie Wehunt

Teacher & Coach

https://www.facebook.com/profile.php?id=100002340907098

My name is Carrie Sokolowski Wehunt. I am a mother of three children - Dalton, Hayden Claire, and Grayson. I've been a teacher for 24 years and coached many sports for middle and high school students. I played three sports at Juniata College and was inducted into the Sports Hall of Fame in October 2013 for Softball, Field Hockey, and Women's basketball. I was a personal trainer for years empowering women to become stronger mentally and physically so they may enjoy their lives to the fullest.

I love spending time with my kids cheering them on. I owe all my accomplishments and life achievements to GOD, family, and friends. "And now these three remain – Faith, Hope and Love, but the greatest of these is love. – Corinthians 13:13"

I love writing books and sharing with others my personal journey that never ends it only gets better with each season of LIFE.

My Neverending Story

By Carrie Wehunt

The Library Lion by Michelle Knudsen, illustrated by Kevin Hawkes, is a charming picture book that tells the story of a lion who loves to visit the library and learns several lessons along the way. Important lessons learned in a library:

Good Behavior—"The lion loved the library. He loved the books, and he loved the librarian, and he loved the quiet."

Respect the rules—"But then the lion roared. And he roared so loudly that the librarian had to put her hands over her ears."

Take Care of the Books—"The lion was very helpful. He helped to find lost books, and he dusted the shelves, and he carried the books back to the library."

Always show kindness—"When the lion had to leave the library, everyone came to say goodbye. The librarian gave him a big hug, and the children gave him a big cheer."

THE END - Wasn't that a great story, boys and girls?

"Ms. Carrie, did you always want to be a librarian? Did you always like reading books because I don't like reading?" Ha - my heart chuckles at the innocence of a child.

A child's ability to speak their minds without filters or hesitation, expressing their most intimate thoughts and feelings openly and honestly. Their laughter and smiles are infectious, emanating from a place of unbridled happiness and delight in simple pleasures. Children marvel in awe at the smallest things—it could be a butterfly flying around aimlessly, a rainbow after the most horrific storm, a puddle that creates frustration for others—always finding magic and wonder in everyday moments even if it is listening to a story read or told. Sitting cross-legged on the floor, completely absorbed in hearing a story, oblivious to the world around them as they journey through the pages of a captivating story being read to them. Hanging on every word connecting the message from page to page, and intricately breaking down every color, line, and image in the illustrations that go with the words they are hearing. Watching, waiting, and then wanting more.

"A book is a dream that you hold in your hand." - Neil Gaiman

When I was little, one of my favorite places to go was the library. The place where the air smelled like freshly printed paper and the crinkling of the clear protective wrap from books being opened. The shelves stretched up so high as if they could touch the sky, and every book sparkled and shined with different colors and images. As I gazed around the room I felt like the books were whispering secrets just waiting for me to discover them. Books that contained doors to different worlds—mysteries waiting to be solved, love stories to sigh over, friendship drama to be resolved, or magic spells waiting to transport me to faraway lands. Staking a claim in the cozy corners on a bean bag or cushion. If I needed help, the librarian always smiled kindly offering gentle guidance and recommendations for new adventures or reading aloud one of the adventures she would choose from the neverending shelves of books. Her voice was soft, loud, strong, silly—simply magical with every word, emotion, or character constantly creating a movie in my mind and bringing the book to life.

Every time I came home from a trip to the library, I transformed my room into my own library—placing pillows in the corner to have a reading nook, shelves displaying rows of books neatly arranged by size, genre, colorful covers, and whimsical illustrations; chapter books filled with daring adventures and fantastical tales. I created barcodes that were taped to the back of every book and a checkout station for those who wanted to borrow one of my adventures (not sure who I thought was coming to borrow a book?). Every time someone entered my room, they needed to be "quiet" because it was a library—my dream as a child was to someday read books to children.

"When you wish upon a star, it makes no difference who you are. Anything your heart desires will come to you." - Pinnochio

As I got older, my interests changed as often things do while navigating the craziness of middle school and high school. My love of sports took over and I spent every moment on a ball field, basketball court, or playing pick-up games with friends. My love for books never went away, just placed on the back burner making room for other passions and dreams. In my spare time, I babysat for neighbors, helped out at the neighborhood pool with swim lessons, and jumped in assisting at summer camps. Everything was always centered around my love for children. Children inspire love through their resilience, imagination, and ability to see the world with wonder and optimism. I wanted to be someone who played a vital role in shaping children and future generations. To be someone who makes a profound impact on the lives of children—to inspire, guide, and empower young minds, helping them learn and grow academically, socially, physically, and emotionally. I wanted to be a teacher!

At Juniata College, I found ways to pursue my love for teaching, mentoring, and inspiring kids of all ages outside of my classes and requirements for a teaching degree. I was a lifeguard on campus for homeschooled children as well as a group of Down syndrome children who came to enjoy the pure excitement and bliss of splashing in the water. I was president of JC Outreach—a community service-based club that reaches out to the community around the college. I invited and organized Pennsylvania's chapter for Special Olympics to take place on our campus using our facilities and space, but most importantly allowing college students an opportunity to mentor, encourage, support, and inspire athletes in a manner they don't often get to do. I did outside tutoring for local children struggling with their learning and found more often than not it was helping them to learn how to read. What a joy it was to teach kids how to read so they can enjoy books—my heart was overjoyed.

"I believe the children are our future, teach them well and let them lead the way. Show them all the beauty they possess inside, give them a sense of pride to make it easier. Let the children's laughter remind us how we used to be." - Whitney Houston

After graduation, I went home to find a teaching job. I was beyond thrilled to receive an offer from a local private school teaching first grade—I get to teach kids how to read! I was teaching alongside some amazing teachers of all ages and experiences. I loved all my students, their parents, and the unending opportunities to inspire and encourage the future. One of the greatest moments within teaching is experiencing the "aha" or lightbulb moments when students grasp a concept or make a meaningful connection. This moment often symbolizes a breakthrough in understanding and confidence for the student, and it brings immense joy and satisfaction to a teacher. It's a powerful reminder of the impact teachers have in shaping their students' learning journeys and helping them succeed academically and personally. These moments affirm a teacher's dedication, passion, and commitment to making a positive difference in the lives of children and their students. Teaching is an opportunity to be a source of inspiration and motivation to continuously foster growth and learning in young minds.

Several years into my teaching, I was given the most amazing opportunity to become a founder of a new Catholic School that was starting in my area. Blessed! I was one of four teachers and a principal that served as the foundation for the learning that would take place at this school. We worked diligently and collaboratively creating our school policies, our vision, our mission, our curriculum, and many other exciting components that go into starting a new educational journey. After the first year of teaching first grade, my principal asked me to follow her to a different part of the new building that had not been occupied with students or activities. We stood in the doorway of the largest space I had seen. She looked at me and said, "I want you to build me a library! Do you think you can do it?" Me? A library?? Yes, yes, yes!!

I get to create a place specifically designed to engage young minds and foster a love of reading and learning. To me a children's library serves so many purposes: Support students' academic needs by providing information, facilitating research, and encouraging independent study; cultivate a love of reading and literacy among students; offer a world of imagination, learning, discovery, foster intellectual curiosity, and provide opportunities for social interaction and personal growth in a nurturing environment. I got couches, fun chairs, rugs, bookshelves, computers, tables, and colorful artwork that hung on the walls and from the ceiling. The once-empty space was transformed into a place of magic and wonder.

"I have always imagined that Paradise will be a kind of library."
- Jorge Luis Borges, an Argentine writer and poet

During this time, I had begun having kids of my own. I was so excited and over the moon to be a mom, after all, being a mom is the greatest teaching job to ever be given. With a career opportunity for my former husband, we moved to a place, which allowed me to be a stay-at-home mom. I had the opportunity to teach empathy, kindness, respect, and responsibility through everyday interactions as well as the highest role model demonstrating resilience, perseverance, and problem-solving skills, a love for learning, curiosity about the world, and a desire for personal growth and achievement.

Another career opportunity presented itself which meant another move to another state and school. The school we were becoming a part of was fairly new and hadn't had the opportunity to create a library. Guess what? I can do it! I spent several conversations with the Head of School allowing me to start a library even if it was occupying a small closet space. I had the knowledge and background and excitement to do it. After receiving the green light, I purchased a library computer system that allowed me to barcode and categorize books with our school's name. I asked families within the school for donations and spent time during my youngest nap time and in the evenings when my kids were sleeping. I was so happy to be creating another place where children can touch, smell, and explore new adventures and ideas. The idea of the library grew from a closet to a small room and then to a large space with a librarian—guess who it was? Yep, me! I was ecstatic to be asked to step into this role and teach library skills to students ranging from two-year-olds through fourth grade. I immediately began to create a curriculum that was enriching and foundational for children's lifelong learning of books in a library.

"Libraries store the energy that fuels the imagination. They open up windows to the world and inspire us to explore and achieve, and contribute to improving our quality of life." - Sidney Sheldon

"Libraries are not just about books, they are about freedom of the mind." - David Starkey

During these years of teaching, I was also raising my children. I was creating adventures of my own with and through my children. I became the storyteller at bedtime—inventing magical worlds with my children as explorers and superheroes; I became the environmental tour guide exploring playgrounds within a 30-minute radius, hiking trails that took us through areas filled with animals; I became the baker who provided delicious treats for special occasions; I became Picasso's mom supplying every paint, paintbrush, play-doh, crayons and markers for my children to create and design; I became a leader in establishing family traditions and cultural awareness; I became my children's mentor, cheerleader, spiritual leader, but most importantly I became their "safe place."

Life is like a BOOK.

We write our own books every day where the chapters are telling the story of our lives. Each chapter has its own theme, challenges, and growth. Each chapter has a shift in our storyline such as transitions from one phase to another—infancy to childhood to adolescence to young adults. Each chapter represents a phase where we learn from mistakes, praise our successes and accomplishments, resolve issues or overcome challenges, and thank our Lord for the unconditional blessings that we experienced. What we experience in one chapter often influences the next.

Cover and Title: The cover of a book is its identity, a reader's first impression—much like our own outside persona and how others perceive us. The title symbolizes the theme of the book—our title is our purpose in life. It reflects our core identity, aspirations, and the narrative we want to convey to others.

Chapters: A book is divided into chapters just like our lives are marked by distinct phases. Each chapter represents a different stage in our lives—some are good, some are bad, some are happy, and some are sad.

Plot Development: The plot of a book encompasses the development of the characters and storylines. The plot of our lives includes our personal growth, achievements, and the challenges we face. Conflict and resolution play a part in a story mirroring the obstacles and triumphs we encounter in our everyday lives.

Characters: A book features a variety of characters who influence the protagonist's journey, our lives are shaped by the people around us—family, friends, mentors, and colleagues. Every character's interaction with others contributes to the richness of the story as well in our lives, relationships play a crucial role in shaping our personal growth and personal experiences.

Setting: The setting of a book provides the places in which the story unfolds. The setting in our lives includes the physical environment, cultural background, and societal influences. These play a part in shaping our perspectives, interactions, challenges, and achievements.

Plot twists and Turns: Just like a book has unexpected twists, so does our lives. There are surprises and unexpected, unforeseen events that alter our plans, dreams, and goals.

Epilogue: An epilogue provides a final reflection of the story. Reflecting on past chapters for insight and wisdom, and appreciating the journey. In our lives, the legacy we leave behind as well as the impact we have on others may be our personal epilogue.

Continuation: A book may have a final ending, but life continues beyond the pages. New chapters represent a continuation of our story, filled with new opportunities, challenges, and experiences.

"The joy of life comes from our encounters with new experiences, and hence there is no greater joy than to have an endlessly changing horizon, for each day to have a new and different sun." - Into the Wild (2007)

So what would my book look like?

My book would have a picture of my kids and me on a couch surrounded by colorful books of all sizes. There are rainbows and unicorns on the walls behind us. They embody hope, magic, purity, and uniqueness. There is a never-ending smile on our faces and a light in our eyes. And just like a cover, my arms are around them always offering protection and security.

My chapters are filled with moments and memories that will always bring me back "home" in my heart—each birth, first steps, first words, the start of school, riding a bike, tying a shoe, field trips, sports, dances, sleepovers, achievements, driving a car, graduations, and first day of college. Each chapter has a beginning and an ending weaving through twists and turns that include happiness, joy, laughter, success, thankfulness, blessings, loss, hurt, fear, doubt, pain, and confusion. Life never stops, always moving forward, turning page after page. Just like recalling a memory, with a book one can go back and reread certain chapters to remember, to learn, and to relive.

There are so many characters that play a part in my story—my family, my friends, my colleagues, my mentors, my church, my students, my teachers, and my coaches—all perfectly placed to challenge me on every page and every chapter along the way.

"Life is a journey, not a destination. The story is in the journey."
- Ralph Waldo Emerson

Eddie Pinero said "The book can be unwritten if you hold the pen. When you fall, promise to get back up; when you get misplaced, remember getting lost is how you find yourself; when you're scared, know the dark is before dawn; these are the stairs that will take you higher. Tiredness is not defeated; wandering is not lost; vulnerability is not weakness; mistakes are not defining; hardship is not a deterrent—these are the pages in the story you are writing. And it's the story of a lifetime."

In every lesson (I have learned), I want my kids and my students to know:

- Reflect and Grow
- Capture the Moments
- Embrace the Journey
- Always Go Forward
- Find Your Perspective

- Appreciate the Characters
- See the Big Picture

EVERY STORY MATTERS—read the books, find the magic, take the adventures, stay until the end, and share with others the beauty inside!

Kimberly Tyler

https://www.linkedin.com/in/kimberly-tyler-a8849539/
https://www.facebook.com/kimberly.tyler.161
https://www.instagram.com/kimmijotyler
https://www.brokenvesselholylight.com/

Kimberly Tyler M.Ed is a seasoned educator and leader with over 30 years in education and children's ministry leadership. A retired Special Education Director and dedicated teacher, she possesses a wealth of knowledge and experience in supporting students with diverse needs, advocating for inclusive practices, and fostering positive learning environments. Kimberly is a compassionate author with a profound gift for seeing others succeed despite any challenges that they may face. Residing in Northern California with her husband and extended family, she draws inspiration from the beautiful surroundings and close-knit community. Kimberly's writing reflects her genuine desire to uplift and empower readers as she shares stories that resonate with faith, hope, and resilience. Her unique blend of storytelling and encouragement has positively impacted the hearts of readers worldwide. An accomplished creative, her favorite mediums are fabric arts such as quilting and embroidery. She can be found at www.brokenvesselholylight.com

Unquenchable Joy

By Kimberly Tyler

Life's daily and long-term goals and visions can be compelling and uplifting, full of hope and promise, leading us to plan and expand our horizons and dreams. I love to set visions, plan for tomorrow, and make audacious goals; the bigger, the better. It energizes me and gives me a sense of joyful purpose. I also identify with people who dream big and love to hear of their accomplishments and victories. But I can also experience a sense of failure and disappointment when I fall short of my own goals or the ones the world has set for me. I have realized I am not alone in that.

For women navigating the complexities of modern life and its pressures, the pursuit of joy can often feel elusive. However, the Bible presents a profound truth: Actual, lasting joy is not a fleeting emotion but an unquenchable force that provides energy, enthusiasm, and the foundation for lasting happiness. By embracing biblical principles and wholeheartedly following Jesus Christ's commandments, I have found that it is possible to cultivate a joy-filled life that endures and thrives even in the face of adversity.

As a friend and sister, let me share the secret to unquenchable joy: a deep, personal relationship with Jesus Christ. This relationship is not just a distant acquaintance but an intimate connection that transforms our hearts and minds. Jesus Himself invites us into this relationship, promising abundant, lasting joy. In John 15:11, He says, "I have told you this so that my joy may be in you and that your joy may be complete."

This joy is not dependent on external circumstances but flows from knowing and being known by the Creator of the universe. When we draw near to Jesus, we experience His presence, which fills us with an indescribable and glorious joy (1 Peter 1:8). This unquenchable joy then becomes our strength, as Nehemiah 8:10 declares, "The joy of the Lord is your strength."

Jesus' joy is not like the fleeting happiness the world gives. It is deep, abiding, and unquenchable. It sustains us through life's highs and lows, energizing us with enthusiasm and hope. This joy is a powerful force that can transform our lives, making us resilient and capable of facing any challenge with a positive outlook.

As we align our lives with biblical principles, we begin to be established in unquenchable joy and see ourselves rooted in it more deeply each day. These principles are not burdensome rules but life-giving truths that guide us into God's perfect will. Psalm 19:8 affirms, "The precepts of the Lord are right, giving joy to the heart." By living according to God's Word, we position ourselves to receive His blessings and experience His energizing joy. There are several simple but foundational daily practices we can focus on to help cultivate and apply these truths to our lives.

Gratitude: Cultivating a heart of gratitude is a powerful biblical principle that fosters unquenchable joy. In 1 Thessalonians 5:16-18, we are instructed, "Rejoice always, pray continually, give thanks in all circumstances; for this is God's will for you in Christ Jesus." Gratitude reminds us of what we have rather than what we lack, opening our eyes to the countless blessings around us.

Take a moment each day to count your blessings, no matter how small they seem. The practice of gratitude can transform your outlook on life and fill your heart with joy. Write down three things you're thankful for daily, and watch how your perspective changes over time.

Faith is the bedrock of unquenchable joy. Hebrews 11:1 defines faith as "confidence in what we hope for and assurance about what we do not see." Faith allows us to trust in God's promises and find joy in His faithfulness, even when we cannot see the outcome.

Faith: Trust that God's Word is true and His promises are sure. God is always with us, and His presence brings us joy. Psalm 16:11 reminds us, "You make known to me the path of life; you will fill me with joy in your presence, with eternal pleasures at your right hand." No matter where or what we face, we can find joy in knowing God is with us.

God has a unique plan for our lives, and His plans are good. Jeremiah 29:11 promises, "For I know the plans I have for you," declares the Lord, "plans to prosper you and not to harm you, plans to give you hope and a future." Trust that God's plan is unfolding in your life, and find joy in His divine purpose.

Trust: Trusting in God's sovereignty and goodness is another critical principle. Proverbs 3:5-6 exhorts us, "Trust in the Lord with all your heart and lean not on your own understanding; in all your ways submit to him, and he will make your paths straight." Trust replaces anxiety with peace and allows joy to flourish, providing energy and enthusiasm even when life is uncertain.

Trusting God means surrendering our worries and fears to Him. It means believing that He has a plan for our lives and that His plans are good. When we trust God, we can face the future with confidence and joy, knowing He is in control.

Obedience: Obedience to God's commandments is not a restrictive duty but a pathway to unquenchable joy. Jesus said in John 15:10-11, "If you keep my commands, you will remain in my love, just as I have kept my Father's commands and remain in his love. I have told you this so that my joy may be in you and that your joy may be complete." Following Jesus' teachings leads to a fulfilling and joy-filled life.

Obedience to God brings blessings and joy into our lives. When we align our actions with His will, we experience the fullness of His love and happiness. This obedience is not about following rules for the sake of it but about living in harmony with God's perfect plan for us.

One of the most compelling aspects of biblical joy is its resilience and unquenchable nature. Unlike happiness, which can be fleeting and dependent on circumstances, biblical joy endures through trials and tribulations. James 1:2-3 encourages us, "Consider it pure joy, my brothers and sisters, whenever you face trials of many kinds, because you know that the testing of your faith produces perseverance."

Perspective: Viewing challenges through the lens of faith changes our perspective. We understand that God uses trials to refine our character and draw us closer to Him. Romans 5:3-4 reminds us, "Not only so, but we also glory in our sufferings, because we know that suffering produces perseverance; perseverance, character; and character, hope."

When we face difficulties, it can be hard to see their purpose. However, when we trust that God is using these challenges to shape us and make us stronger, we can face them with purpose and joy. Every trial becomes an opportunity for growth and deeper reliance on God.

Presence: God's presence becomes our anchor in difficult times. Psalm 16:11 declares, "You make known to me the path of life; you will fill me with joy in your presence, with eternal pleasures at your right hand." When we feel overwhelmed, turning to God in prayer and worship fills us with His peace and unquenchable joy.

Spending time in God's presence is essential for maintaining unquenchable joy. Whether through prayer, reading the Bible, or worship, these moments of connection with God rejuvenate our spirits and remind us of His unfailing love and faithfulness.

Community: The support of a loving, faith-filled community is vital. Galatians 6:2 urges us, "Carry each other's burdens, and in this way, you will fulfill the law of Christ." Sharing our struggles with fellow believers and receiving their encouragement strengthens our resolve and joy.

We were not meant to walk this journey alone. Being part of a supportive community provides us with encouragement and strength. It reminds us that we are not alone in our struggles and that we have others to lean on. The sense of belonging and the support that comes from the community can greatly enhance our joy.

Daily Devotion: Spend time daily in God's Word and prayer. This intentional practice deepens your relationship with Jesus and grounds you in His promises.

Create a sacred space in your home where you can retreat daily to connect with God. Whether it's a quiet corner with a comfortable chair and a Bible or a serene spot in your garden, having a dedicated place for your devotion time helps make it a consistent habit.

Worship: Make worship a regular part of your life. Whether through singing, movement, or quiet reflection, worship shifts your focus to God's greatness and goodness, fueling your joy. Worship is a powerful way for us to express our thankfulness to God. It lifts our spirits and fills us with His presence. By finding ways to incorporate worship into our daily routine, whether through music, art, or simply meditating on God's goodness, we can invite His spirit into our environment, hearts, and souls.

Service: Serving others brings joy. Acts 20:35 quotes Jesus saying, "It is more blessed to give than to receive." Look for opportunities to bless others with your time, talents, and resources.

Serving others not only blesses them but also brings immense joy to our lives. Our own problems diminish as we experience the joy of having made a positive impact on the lives of others.

Rest: Prioritize rest and self-care. God designed us to need rest, and taking time to recharge physically, emotionally, and spiritually is essential for maintaining unquenchable joy. My greatest periods of discouragement happen when I am tired; rest can help restore my optimism. In our busy lives, it's easy to neglect rest. However, rest is crucial for our well-being.

Take time to relax, enjoy nature, read a good book, or spend time with loved ones. When we are well-rested, we are better able to experience and maintain joy. Our bodies are temples of the Holy Spirit (1 Corinthians 6:19-20), and caring for them is an act of stewardship. Feeling physically well makes us more equipped to experience and sustain joy.

Creative Expression: Engage in innovative activities that bring you joy, whether painting, writing, crafting, or gardening. Creativity is a beautiful way to express and experience joy. Even if it's just doodling with a pen, let your creativity be an outlet to connect with the Creator. God is the ultimate Creator, and as beings made in His image, we find joy in creating. Embrace your creative gifts and use them to glorify God and enhance your happiness.

These daily practices provide us with the unquenchable joy, enthusiasm, and energy to achieve our goals and see our visions come to pass. They also sustain us through the dark and challenging times we all face. I have found that during these times, the closeness of the Lord helped me and strengthened me, and He showed me in the midst of it that joy is always within reach, no matter what challenges we walk through.

I remember a time when life felt overwhelmingly difficult. My family was going through a crisis, and I was struggling to find peace because the stress and anxiety were almost unbearable. But amid this turmoil, I decided to start a gratitude journal. Each day, I wrote down three things I was thankful for, no matter how small. It was amazing how this simple practice transformed my outlook. I began to see God's blessings even in the smallest details of my life. This shift in perspective brought a deep sense of joy and peace despite the ongoing challenges.

I have also walked through a season in my life when I faced a severe health scare. I was told I had a terminal illness for which there was no approved treatment and to get my affairs in order. I was lucky enough to have a group of praying sisters surround me, and I was able to be enrolled in an experimental drug treatment program. I am happy to say the treatment was successful and also paved the way for a new treatment for those with this disease. Still, the treatment side effects were terrible, and the entire ordeal went on for almost 2 years with no real idea if it would be successful or not during the treatment.

The uncertainty and fear of what the future held were overwhelming. During this time, I clung to Proverbs 3:5-6, trusting in God's plan and His goodness. I prayed for healing and strength and surrounded myself with supportive friends and family who prayed with me. This experience taught me to trust God more deeply, and His peace and joy sustained me. Even in the face of uncertainty, I found joy in knowing that God was in control and His plans for me were good.

Throughout times of personal struggle such as this, the support of a loving community has been a lifeline for me. Being part of a faith-filled community has shown me the power of shared burdens and joy. When I faced the loss of my sister, my church community surrounded me with love, prayers, and practical support. They carried my burdens and reminded me of God's promises. Their encouragement and presence brought comfort and a sense of joy during a challenging time.

Living in unquenchable joy is not a one-time event but a daily journey. It requires intentionality and a commitment to nurturing our relationship with God. Here are some additional practical steps to help you cultivate immense, unquenchable joy in your everyday life:

Celebrate Small Victories: Acknowledge and celebrate even the smallest achievements. Each step forward is a reason to rejoice.

Speak Life: Use your words to uplift and encourage yourself and others. Speaking positive and faith-filled words can transform your mindset and atmosphere.

Stay Connected: Stay connected with fellow believers who can support and encourage you. Regular fellowship and accountability are essential for maintaining joy.

Pray Without Ceasing: Maintain an ongoing conversation with God throughout your day. Prayer keeps you connected to His presence and allows His joy to flow through you.

Life is full of different seasons, each with its own challenges and blessings. Embracing these seasons with a heart full of joy can help us navigate them with grace and strength. Ecclesiastes 3:1 reminds us, "There is a time for everything, and a season for every activity under the heavens." Seasons come and go, but there are several that we may see as we pursue our visions and goals. Recognizing and embracing each season fuels our unquenchable joy and builds our relationship with God. Some of the common ones we may see are:

Season of Waiting: Waiting can be one of the hardest seasons to endure. Whether waiting for a job, a relationship, or a breakthrough, it can be easy to lose hope. But remember, God is at work even in the waiting. Psalm 27:14 encourages us, "Wait for the Lord; be strong and take heart and wait for the Lord." Trust that God's timing is perfect, and find joy in knowing He is in control.

Season of Growth: Growth can be painful as it often involves stretching and challenging us in new ways. During these times, embrace the process and trust that God is molding you into His image. James 1:4 says, "Let perseverance finish its work so that you may be mature and complete, not lacking anything." Find joy in the growth and transformation God is bringing about in your life.

Season of Harvest: Harvest seasons are filled with blessings and abundance. These are times to celebrate and give thanks for God's provision. Psalm 126:5-6 says, "Those who sow with tears will reap with songs of joy. Those who go out weeping, carrying seed to sow, will return with songs of joy, carrying sheaves with them." Rejoice in the harvest and share your blessings with others.

Season of Rest: Rest is essential to our journey. God commands us to rest and recharge. Matthew 11:28-29 invites us, "Come to me, all you who are weary and burdened, and I will give you rest. Take my yoke upon you and learn from me, for I am gentle and humble in heart, and you will find rest for your souls." Embrace rest as a time to be refreshed and renewed in God's presence.

As we walk through our life and all its seasons, our unquenchable joy can be a powerful witness to others. When people see the joy of the Lord in our lives, even under challenging circumstances, they are drawn to the source of that joy. Matthew 5:16 encourages us, "In the same way, let your light shine before others, that they may see your good deeds and glorify your Father in heaven." Let your joy be a testimony of God's love and grace.

Unquenchable joy has the power to transform our lives and the lives of those around us. It is a powerful and undisputable testimony of God's goodness and faithfulness. When we live with Unquenchable Joy, we reflect God's light to the world. Life will always have its ups and downs, but we don't have to navigate it alone.

Jesus is the source of unquenchable joy that will see you through every trial and triumph. His joy is your strength, hope, and foundation for lasting happiness. As you lean into Him, remember you are loved, valued, and never alone; let your life be a testament to the unquenchable joy that comes from knowing Jesus. Share this joy with others, and let it be a beacon of hope and encouragement. Together, let's live out the unquenchable joy that He so generously gives and watch as it transforms our lives and the lives of those around us.

Sheree Wertz

Dental Hygiene 411
Dental Hygienist & Myofunctional Therapist

https://www.linkedin.com/in/sheree-wertz-43b71a46/
https://www.facebook.com/groups/healthymouthmoms
https://www.instagram.com/dental_hygiene_411/
https://shereewertz.com
https://shereewertz.com/myo

Sheree Wertz is a dedicated mom, dental hygienist and myofunctional therapist with a passion for empowering families to take control of their health and wellbeing. With years of experience in the dental field, Sheree has developed a deep understanding of the critical role oral health plays in overall wellness. Her journey led her to specialize in myofunctional therapy, a niche that allows her to address issues related to breathing, sleep, and oral function.

Everyone has the potential to live their best life and thrive by taking ownership of their health. Sheree's work involves making a difference in people's lives through improved health and increased awareness, empowering families to take action and tweak habits that impact their daily life. Her personalized care and dedication make her a standout in her field, inspiring her families to embrace a healthier, more vibrant lifestyle with her SHIFT method. Shift your perspective… Simple Habit Incentives For Transformation. To learn more about Sheree Wertz and how she can help you enhance your overall wellness.

Tame your thoughts and your tongue
If you believe you can or you believe you can't, you are right...

By Sheree Wertz

Knowledge is a very important tool for positive change. The more knowledge we have, the better choices we can make to live a healthier life. A happy, healthy life starts from the top down with your mind, your thoughts, your beliefs, how you breathe, and respecting the one body you get. You are your greatest asset and your best investment to living your best life.

It's easy to ignore what we don't understand. To tell you the truth, for the first 20+ years of my adult life, that's what I did.

If I didn't understand it or did not want to deal with something, I ignored it. Once I realized that by not feeling the feelings and dealing with the thing, I was only hurting myself, the saying above changed my perspective. I had a series of things happen in my life that were all out of my control—decisions others made that had a profound effect on my life.

I was told I would not have children. I had several miscarriages, people close to me passed, I got divorced, I had breast cancer. What I learned from these experiences is that it is not what happens in your life, it is how you process what happens, how you see it, and how you react that makes the difference.

I put others' wants and needs before my own for many years, to the point that someone told me I had a broken wanter. What did that even mean? I wanted things for sure. However, he was right I had no idea what I really wanted out of this life I was living. I was just getting through each day with no real plan and no end goal.

I believed I would have a child. After the initial shock of things life threw at me, I made a conscious choice to pick up and keep going.

Happiness is a choice. Not an easy one sometimes, but nevertheless, it is a choice.

What I realized is that you are your greatest asset and investment in life. You have to make yourself happy and healthy. No one else is going to do that for you. In order to do that you need to know yourself, date yourself, ask yourself what you want and what will make you happy. I was 45 years old when I got divorced, and I had no idea what I wanted.

I had to start over. I still did not put myself first. Until I was diagnosed with Cancer. This created the biggest shift in my life. Do not do what I did and wait for the wake-up call.

You are the one and only **OWNER**.

Self-care and self-respect are not selfish, they are essential.

You cannot pour from an empty cup.

You must meet your basic needs first in order to thrive!

I started with the basics. We don't even realize we are struggling with meeting these basic needs.

O.W.N.E.R stands for Oxygen, Water, Nutrition, Enough Sleep, and Respecting the one body you get.

We are given shelter, food, and clothing as a child. Many of us are not taught to put ourselves and our health first when growing up. We are taught to feed ourselves, potty trained, and how to shower and brush our teeth. Beyond that, depending on our parents' beliefs, we are taught we need to provide for our future family. We are taught to work hard, save money, and repeat the cycle.

We are taught to drive, we are taught how to put in gas, take it through the car wash, take it for oil changes, rotate the tires, and maintain it, so it will continue to get us where we want to go. But what about maintaining our bodies? We will all have more than one car in a lifetime, and we spend more time maintaining a car that can be replaced than we do caring for a body we will be in our entire lives. We only get one body. Doesn't it make sense to put ourselves first before anything else, especially before something we won't even have our whole life and that can be replaced if needed?

Our body has 11 major organ systems, all working together as a whole for our health and wellness. Traditional health care treats symptoms and each system separately. Understanding how all the systems in the body work together is crucial for achieving total health.

The human body is a complex, interconnected network where each system—respiratory, circulatory, digestive, nervous, and more—depends on and influences the others. For example, proper breathing not only ensures efficient oxygen delivery to cells but also affects sleep quality, stress levels, and even oral health. Acknowledging this interconnectedness helps us ask better questions and seek comprehensive solutions rather than treating symptoms in isolation. By considering the body as a whole, we can identify the root causes of health issues, implement more effective preventive measures, and achieve a balanced, thriving state of wellness.

The first thing we do when we are born is take a breath, through our nose; the last thing we do when we die is take a breath, usually a gasp through our mouth.

When we talk about being healthy, we should start with how we breathe! Do you primarily use your mouth or your nose?

This is important because we are meant to breathe through our nose, not our mouth. Breathing through our mouth throws everything out of balance in our body. We are lucky as humans that we have the option to breathe through our mouth when our nose is not an option. However, we are not as healthy, and we will probably live a shorter unhealthy life.

When we breathe through our mouth, we get 18% less oxygen to our brain and body; we lose 40% of our water when we sleep. Our circadian rhythm is disrupted when we sleep, leading to an increase in blood pressure and cortisol, which then makes us crave sugar and put on weight around the midsection. Disrupted sleep creates a lack of focus, energy, and motivation. It is a vicious cycle.

I had frequent sore throats and nosebleeds as a child. I was given an antibiotic that stained my teeth, I was made fun of for many years, which affected how I felt about myself. I sucked my thumb for 12 years, my daughter sucked her fingers, and we both wet the bed into double digits. I did not see the correlation to breathing until it became a social issue for her.

Where your tongue is positioned, how you hold it and how it functions has a huge effect on our health when we are growing up.

It was not until I had a child of my own I understood how important breathing was to growth and development. How this had an effect on me looking back and how it is affecting others that do not have this information.

How we breathe has an effect on how we look, the shape of our face, how we feel, how we sleep, and how healthy we are overall. The diagram shows the difference between a mouth breather and a nasal breather.

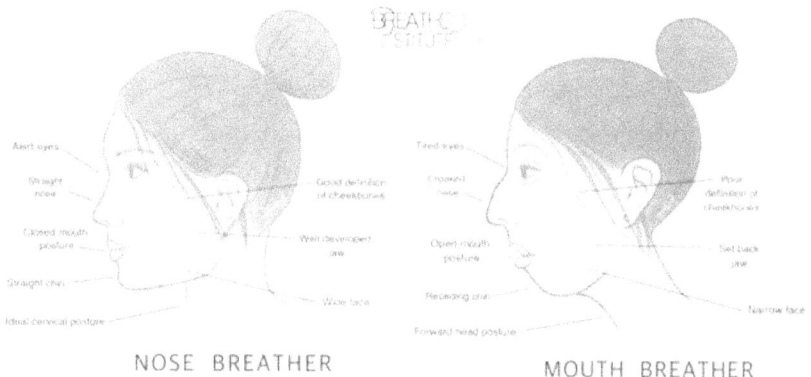

NOSE BREATHER   MOUTH BREATHER

Every single breath is an opportunity to nourish our bodies, calm our minds, and enhance our health. It starts when we are born. Did you know that babies breathe through their noses until about 3–4 months? This is where we should start.

How we breathe, and the position of our tongue play crucial roles in impacting everything from our growth and development to our sleep to our quality of life. By understanding and optimizing our basic needs, we can truly transform our lives. Let's take a deep breath.

Breathing is fundamental to our existence, and its impact on our health and longevity is so underestimated and under-discussed.

Breathing is more than just an automatic process; it's a vital component of our health that influences our physical, mental, and emotional well-being.

I am a dental hygienist turned myofunctional therapist after what my daughter went through. My husband was a dentist, and his father was an orthodontist. We were not taught to look at the position of the tongue and the effect it has on function, eating, speaking, breathing, growth and development, sleep, focus, behavior, and health.

I was told my daughter would outgrow bed-wetting; she did not outgrow it, she grew into difficulty focusing and behavioral issues due to lack of sleep. Fifteen years ago, the doctor thought I was crazy when I told him my daughter was sleep-deprived.

Bed-wetting is a common issue in young children. However, when it persists beyond the typical age of outgrowing it (usually around 5–7 years old), it can be a sign of underlying issues. Despite various interventions, with my daughter, her bed-wetting continued beyond the expected age.

Chronic bed-wetting in older children is often a source of embarrassment and stress for both the child and their parents.

We spent thousands of dollars seeing the wrong doctor because I thought it was a bladder issue; I now know it was a breathing issue.

A sleep study revealed that her breathing was frequently interrupted during the night, preventing her from entering deep, restorative sleep. This disruption was the root cause of her bed-wetting and behavioral symptoms, not ADHD.

Breathing through our noses is critical for our health and how our bodies are meant to operate.

Our nose has many functions. It warms, filters out particles, dust, and allergens, humidifies inhaled air, and produces nitric oxide.

Mouth breathing, especially at a young age, can dramatically change the growth, development and structure of a child's face. Their body is in fight-or-flight mode when they sleep. It's the brain that tells the body to get rid of anything it does not need, so it empties the bladder.

While bed-wetting, snoring and grinding are signs and can be a nuisance, disruption of REM sleep drops your cognitive ability for the next day by 35%. Symptoms of sleepiness include fatigue, irritability, lack of motivation, focus or concentration, frequent illness, weight gain, high blood pressure, anxiety, depression and more.

According to the National Institute of Health, 1 in 3 Americans are not getting enough sleep.

Sleeping with your mouth open consistently is often a sign of a sleep disorder. There are more than 90 diagnosable disorders. I did not know that until I did research for this chapter. These can include sleep apnea, insomnia, bed-wetting, restless leg syndrome, and more.

Sleep apnea in children is becoming more and more prevalent. It is estimated that 10–20% of children have nighttime breathing disorders. Unfortunately, an estimated 90% are undiagnosed or misdiagnosed. Like my daughter was.

Children undergoing evaluation for ADHD should be screened for sleep disorders.

Proper diagnosis and treatment can alleviate not only the physical symptoms but also the emotional and psychological stress associated with chronic bed-wetting.

Untreated children grow into adults with sleep issues; it is estimated more than 50 million of them.

Sleeping disorders can contribute to serious health issues like heart failure, diabetes, and obesity.

Health and wealth are right under our noses. By focusing on these foundational aspects, we can improve not only our own lives but also the lives of our children.

Our healthcare system treats symptoms once we have a problem. But what if there were warning signs we could look for in our children before there is a problem?

Functional breathing in childhood helps to create foundations for life-long health and correct structural development. Many children have breathing issues or dysfunctions that are often overlooked or dismissed as unimportant.

Poor breathing can have negative effects on many aspects of a child's health and well-being.

The good news is that once the causes of a child's breathing issues are addressed, poor breathing habits and incorrect muscle function can often be corrected through breathing exercises and functional retraining of orofacial muscles and posture.

Signs that a child's breathing may need an evaluation

Mouth breathing, frequent colds, dark circles under the eyes, part or present Asthma, runny nose, blocked nose, teeth grinding, snoring, restless sleep, bed-wetting, crooked teeth, no spaces between baby teeth, picky eating.

Causes of breathing dysfunction

Functional breathing issues in children can start due to allergy, asthma, or enlarged adenoids and tonsils. Other common causes of breathing and airway problems in children include gastro-esophageal reflux, prematurity, newborn breathing difficulty, not enough space for the tongue, and tongue tie.

These can lead to stress, trauma, and emotional issues, which also can play a role. These causes need to be adequately addressed, with attention from appropriate health professionals.

The role of breathing and orofacial muscle retraining

Dysfunctional or abnormal breathing behaviors can become an undiagnosed issue. Breathing exercises and mind-mouth-body practices can help restore functional breathing and break these vicious cycles. Orofacial myofunctional exercises are often needed in addition to breathing retraining to correct oral muscle and tongue function.

Dysfunction can lead to restriction of the airway and has many serious consequences. Some children's airways can be restricted to the size of a straw—imagine trying to breathe through a straw and how much stress it would cause you as an adult. Sleep apnea becomes common at this age, and tongue restriction and low tongue posture are both indicative of sleep and breathing problems.

You can also observe changes in the body posture which are due to airway issues. Typical body posture from airway issues will be with the shoulders slightly rolled and the head forward. Open mouth breathing is common in children—if your child always has their mouth open when at rest, this indicates myofunctional issues and will affect facial growth.

Myofunctional therapy can be of great help to correct issues while the child is still growing and prevent them from needing braces in the future. We are told to wait til our children are 7 or 8 for traditional braces. 80% of growth and development of the dental arch has happened by then and there is a very high relapse rate of 90%, so most children's teeth will revert back to bad positioning over time. Especially if the dysfunction had not been addressed.

If myofunctional therapy is started before or alongside braces, it can help reduce this relapse rate by fixing the underlying issue.

The problem with braces is that they treat the symptom of the problem (crooked teeth) without fixing the underlying cause: incorrect positioning of the tongue and incorrect swallowing.

If you notice that your child has any of the above symptoms, consider dealing with the root of the problem through myofunctional therapy. If your child has already had braces, but you can see signs of relapse, like teeth not fitting together properly, then myofunctional therapy can help prevent this relapse. The earlier that myofunctional therapy can be started, the better.

Let's take a deep breath, prioritize our breathing, and embark on this journey to do better together, starting with how you think, where your tongue is, and how you breathe.

Investing in yourself and your health is a wise investment. If I can help you, feel free to reach out; I offer a free consultation to ask questions and get answers. If I cannot help, I can point you to someone who can!

www.Shereewertz.com

Lena Khais

Founder and CEO of Atlas Paradigm
Manifestation Coach

https://urlgeni.us/facebook/LenaKhais
https://www.instagram.com/lenakhais
https://atlas-paradigm.com/

Lena Khais is a success and mindset coach who guides her clients on a transformative journey to experience the life they truly desire. Through a blend of neuroscience, spirituality and humor, she effectively demystifies manifestation, breaking it down into easy-to-follow steps that lead to actual results. With a passion of unlocking the potential of human mind, Lena empowers people to attract and live the life by design rather than by default. She teaches how to integrate imagination, focus and emotions to take inspired actions that convert a desire from the blueprint in the mind into the physical reality. What makes her approach unique is her lighthearted and fun take on what you need to step into the world of abundance in alignment with soul's true purpose.

Lena has an advanced degree in Psychology and spent many years in corporate leadership positions working with executive leaders of Fortune 500 to help them craft and crash their goals. After breaking free from her own experience of Groundhog Day, she developed a true passion for coaching others on how to discover their true calling and step into their unapologetically best-self-er version they were born for.

Breaking the Generational Curse
of Money Blocks

By Lena Khais

Understanding Limiting Beliefs Around Money

When I began my journey as a manifestation coach, working with entrepreneurs stuck in the dreaded 4-figure income plateau, I quickly realized that money blocks were at the root of many of their struggles. These limiting beliefs around money often come from deep-rooted, generational patterns. Our ancestors, the way we're raised, and our emotional life experiences shape how we experience and interact with money. But the good news? Beliefs are just thoughts we choose to accept as truth, and that means we have the power to change them.

Generational Inheritance of Money Beliefs

I come from an Eastern European background, where my family's money story runs deep into centuries of working hard for someone else. Money was always scarce, and my ancestors lived with the constant expectation of a rainy day. Saving rather than investing was the norm. My great-grandparents, grandparents, and even my mom all shared the same story—money doesn't come easily, and when it does, you hold onto it for dear life.

Growing up, I often heard, "Money doesn't grow on trees," or "Just be grateful for what you have." These phrases weren't just about budgeting; they were codes for financial fear and scarcity. When you're raised in an environment that views money as something elusive, it shapes your entire approach to earning, saving, and spending.

Many years ago, I remember one afternoon when I sat down with my grandmother to keep her company during her afternoon tea. She had lived through many historical hardships and carried the wisdom of our family's history. I wanted to understand more about these deeply rooted beliefs. In her 90s, she was still sharp as a knife and incredibly insightful.

"Babushka," I began, "can we talk about our family's history? Can you think back to your grandparents? What was it like for them in the late 1800s–early 1900s?"

She looked excited and nostalgic, clearly eager to pass on the baton of generational traditions and wisdom. "Of course, my dear. What do you want to know?"

"I've been thinking a lot lately about how we in our family view money," I said, biting into a biscuit. "You always taught me to save every penny. I remember Grandpa and you always thinking twice about every single purchase, making sure you're considering every possible saving opportunity. It just makes me wonder—where is it coming from? What is the so-called 'story' behind this?"

It didn't take her long to lay it all out for me. "In our family, money was always something uncertain. Your great-grandparents worked so hard, but wars, one after another, destroyed everything they built. Naturally, because of that, they taught us to save because we never knew when the next disaster would come."

What she was sharing made so much sense. I nodded, soaking up her words. "But Babushka, do you think that fear of losing everything has stopped us from taking reasonable risks, from investing in opportunities that could help us grow?"

She pondered this for a moment. "Perhaps, my dear. We were so focused on survival that we couldn't see beyond the immediate needs. It was always about making sure we had enough for tomorrow."

"But times have changed," I suggested gently. "I feel like this mindset has held us back. I'm trying to see money differently—not just something to save, but something to use for growth and abundance."

She smiled, a hint of pride in her eyes. "You are right. We did what we thought was best with what we knew. But you have more opportunities now. If you can use money wisely and without fear, maybe you can break this cycle."

Her words gave me hope. "Thank you. I think it's time we change our story. Not just for me, but for the future generations."

She reached out and squeezed my hand. "I believe in you. Just remember, it's not the money itself, but how you use it and the mindset you carry. If you can change that, you will truly honor our family's struggles by building something greater."

I left our conversation feeling empowered. Understanding where our limiting beliefs came from was the first step in breaking free from them. It was time to create a new legacy—one of abundance, courage, and generational wealth.

Acquiring Money Beliefs Through Experience

Honestly, it took years for me to make that shift. It's not surprising if you think about it. Leaving generational "baggage" aside, even experiences as subtle as watching your parents argue about bills or witnessing a loved one lose their job can leave a mark.

And can we talk about childhood experiences with cartoons and books? Growing up, many of us were captivated by Disney movies and fairy tales, where good always triumphed over evil, and the underdog found their happily ever after. But beneath the enchanting stories and catchy tunes, these tales often sent subtle messages about wealth and morality. A recurring theme in these stories is the portrayal of wealthy characters as villains, leading us to internalize the belief that money is inherently bad and that being rich often means being evil.

Take Cruella De Vil, for instance. She's a quintessential example of how Disney shapes our perception of wealth. Cruella, with her lavish fur coats and rich lifestyle, is the epitome of a boss lady running her own business. But hold on—she's also a puppy-killing maniac! As children, we watched in horror as Cruella schemed to make a fur coat out of adorable Dalmatian puppies. The underlying message? Wealth and success come at the cost of morality and compassion. And let's be honest, it's hard to root for someone who considers puppies as mere fabric.

Then there's the notorious villain, Scar, from *The Lion King*. Though not wealthy in the traditional sense, his desire for power and control mirrors the ruthless corporate mogul archetype. Scar's cunning schemes and willingness to betray his own family to gain the throne display ambition and wealth as synonymous with treachery. He's essentially a corporate raider in a lion's body, leading us to equate the pursuit of power with unethical behavior.

Let's not forget about Ursula from *The Little Mermaid*. With her glamorous yet sinister appearance, Ursula is a savvy businesswoman, dealing in contracts and transactions. However, her manipulative nature of Ariel's dreams for personal gain paints a picture of wealth accumulation through deceit and exploitation. Kids watching this may develop a belief that business savviness and financial success often involve trickery and the suffering of others.

And who could overlook Gaston from *Beauty and the Beast*? While he's not incredibly wealthy, Gaston's self-absorbed pursuit of status and material wealth makes him the quintessential arrogant aristocrat. His character suggests that those who seek riches and recognition are inherently vain and shallow. Plus, anyone who decorates their tavern with antlers is clearly compensating for something, right?

These characters, while entertaining, subtly reinforce the notion that wealth and virtue are mutually exclusive. The message is clear: To be good, one must be modest and unassuming, like Cinderella or Belle, who despite their hardships, remain pure-hearted and honest. On the flip side, wealth and ambition are often depicted as corrupting forces.

It is easy to see how this "solid foundation" taught to us by fictional characters in our early childhood can influence our money beliefs. And then, as we grow older, our own experiences play a significant role, too. I remember my first job as a summer camp counselor. I just came to the United States. I was 19, with no experience, and desperate to make some money. Well, that energy of desperation certainly did its job, no pun intended. I was treated like a disposable thing, overworked, and making "peanuts." It reinforced the belief that making money was hard and that financial stability was always just out of reach.

Another vivid memory is from my early twenties. I had taken a job in a small physician practice, hoping it would lead to a stable career. Instead, I found myself overworked and underpaid, constantly stressed about making ends meet. My boss would remind us how lucky we were to have jobs at all, deepening my belief that financial success was for a select few, and I wasn't one of them.

Changing the Narrative

But there's good news here. The transformative power lies in understanding that a belief is just a thought we choose to accept. By changing our thoughts, we can change our reality.

Let's flip the script with a touch of humor. Imagine if Cruella had a modern rebranding. Instead of a puppy coat mogul, she could be the CEO of a vegan leather company, turning her ambition into ethical entrepreneurship. Picture Scar attending family therapy, resolving his issues with Mufasa, and opening a sanctuary for orphaned lion cubs.

Ursula could pivot to becoming a successful business coach, helping merfolk achieve their dreams without dubious contracts that cost them their voice. Gaston might still decorate with antlers, but he could channel his vanity into a successful lifestyle brand, promoting self-love and body positivity.

The key takeaway here is that while these fairy tales have shaped our early beliefs about money and morality, we can reframe these narratives to create healthier views of wealth. Success doesn't have to come at the expense of our ethics. By recognizing these ingrained stories, we can choose to rewrite our own, where ambition is balanced with compassion, and wealth is a tool for positive change rather than a symbol of greed.

So next time you watch a Disney movie, enjoy the magic but also take a moment to question the underlying messages. After all, in the real world, you can be a successful, wealthy boss without turning into a puppy-killing villain.

My Journey to Abundance

I want to share how learning manifestation and actively working to remove these limiting beliefs allowed me to break the "generational curse" and create a life of abundance.

I remember the exact moment when I decided enough was enough. It was a rainy Tuesday, and I was staring at the balance of my bank account. By then I'd been in corporate jobs for 20 years, working crazy hours, impersonating the infamous hamster running in the wheel, and still living paycheck to paycheck. It finally hit me: If I kept following the same patterns, I'd keep getting the same results. I needed to change my mindset to change my life.

Shortly after, I had a conversation with my friend Heather.

"Heather, do you ever feel like you're fighting against an invisible barrier?"

She laughed, "Only every other day! What's your secret?"

"It's not really a secret," I admitted. "It's about changing how you think about money. Imagine if we put as much energy into manifesting abundance as we do worrying about bills."

Heather's eyes lit up. "You mean, just believe it's possible?"

"Exactly. It's about partnering with the Universe. You wouldn't believe the opportunities that start showing up when you do."

Heather took a sip of her coffee. "Maybe it's time I tried something different."

We both chuckled, knowing that the journey isn't always easy, but the rewards are worth it.

After that conversation, I dove deep into the principles of manifestation. At first, it felt like I was swimming upstream against years of ingrained beliefs. But slowly, things began to shift. I started visualizing success, abundance, and wealth as part of my reality. I wrote affirmations, practiced gratitude, and surrounded myself with positivity.

My breakthrough came when I embraced the idea that the Universe is a partner in creation. The Universe began to deliver in ways that seemed impossible before—royalties from my best-selling book, paid speaking engagements, and the successful coaching business I run today.

Once during a women's networking event, I shared my story with a group of budding entrepreneurs. One of them, Emily, asked, "How do you stay motivated when things get tough?"

"Emily, that's a solid question. And I'd be lying to you if I said that I never have a tough day or a limiting thought that crosses my mind. But

I once read that if plan A doesn't work, the alphabet has 25 more letters. And I've never run into a situation where I needed plan Z."

The room broke out in laughter, but the message was clear. Focus, coupled with a positive mindset, can turn challenges into stepping stones.

Being a mindset and manifestation coach, I can't help myself. I want to share some specific strategies that helped me on this journey:

1. **Visualization and Affirmations**: Every morning, I would spend 10 minutes visualizing my goals as if they had already been achieved. I imagined the joy of financial freedom, the excitement of signing a new coaching client, and the pride of receiving royalties from my book. Alongside this, I repeated affirmations like, "I am a magnet for wealth," and "Money flows to me effortlessly." This daily practice helped rewire my brain to see wealth as a natural part of my life.

2. **Gratitude Practice**: I started a gratitude journal where I wrote down five things I was grateful for each day. This simple practice shifted my focus from what I lacked to what I had. It's incredible how this change in perspective opened up more opportunities for abundance. The more grateful I felt, the more I attracted positive experiences and financial opportunities. And here's one more tip: Write down a couple of things that you don't yet observe in your physical reality. You'd be surprised how quickly you'll attract them into your life.

3. **Surrounding Myself with Positivity**: I consciously chose to spend time with people who had a positive outlook on life and were supportive of my journey. I also filled my environment with books, podcasts, and courses that inspired and motivated me. This positive reinforcement was key in maintaining my new mindset. Honestly, I did not do this alone. I hired a coach

who helped me on this journey. She held the space for me and saw my success on days when I wasn't seeing it. She believed in both of us.

4. **Investing in Myself**: I started seeing money as a tool for growth rather than something to hoard. I invested in courses, coaching, and resources that helped me develop new skills and expand my business. This not only improved my income but also boosted my confidence and self-worth. I also became very intentional with my language. I got rid of words like "debt", "spending", and "wasting money" and focused on "investing", "multiplying", and "growing."

5. **Letting Go of Fear**: One of the biggest hurdles was overcoming the fear of financial insecurity. I learned to trust that the Universe would provide for me. This didn't mean I was reckless with money, but I stopped letting fear dictate my financial decisions. Instead, I made choices from a place of abundance and possibility. Want to try it? Go out to dinner and order whatever you'd like off the menu, without looking at the price. I promise you. You won't bankrupt yourself in one meal. But you will experience the momentum and the taste, no pun intended, of the abundant living.

From Scarcity to Generational Wealth

One of the most significant changes was my approach to money. Instead of saving every penny out of fear, I started investing in myself and my business. I began seeing money as a tool for growth rather than something to hoard. This shift allowed me to create not just a comfortable life for myself but also a foundation for generational wealth.

For instance, investing in my education and personal development opened doors I never imagined. It led to creating courses, writing my books, and speaking at conferences. Each step forward was a testament to the power of shifting my mindset and manifesting abundance.

One pivotal moment in my journey was deciding to invest a significant amount of money into a mindset coach. It was a scary decision, but it turned out to be one of the best investments I ever made. The coach helped me rewire my mindset, open my eyes to new revenue streams, and create growth momentum.

Another key decision was to invest in real estate that felt bigger than my pocket. Coming from a family where saving every penny was the norm, this was a huge leap. But I saw it as an opportunity to build long-term wealth and create a legacy for my children. Our family has "grown into" every house we bought over the years, faster than a toddler outgrows their shoes. The returns from these investments have been remarkable, and they've reinforced my belief in the power of a positive money mindset.

What's Next for YOU

I want to leave you with this: You have the power to transform your relationship with money. By changing your beliefs, you can unlock unlimited potential for creating generational wealth. If you're ready to break through your income plateau and explore how to remove your money blocks, reach out to me. Let's work together to create the life of abundance you deserve.

Remember, the Universe is always ready to deliver—you just need to be open to receiving. Together, we can turn your dreams into reality. Imagine waking up each day with a sense of peace and excitement, knowing that you are in control of your financial destiny. You deserve to live a life of abundance, and it starts with changing your mindset.

If you're feeling stuck, if you're ready to break free from the constraints of your past, if you want to unlock the full potential of your business, we should chat. Let's embark on this journey together. The path to abundance is not just about making more money; it's about transforming your entire relationship with wealth.

You have the power to change your story. You have the power to create a legacy of abundance. Believe in yourself, invest in yourself, and watch as the Universe aligns to support you.

Ana Lucia Martinez, RN

A New Adventure
Peer to Peer Mentor

https://www.linkedin.com/in/anamlv
https://www.facebook.com/anarnclc
https://www.instagram.com/anam.rnclc/
https://www.anewadventurelv.com/
https://calendly.com/anamlv/

Ana is a mom of three beautiful daughters, Registered Nurse, Certified Lactation Counselor, Travel Specialist, and How Money Works Educator. She is an Honors College graduate from the University of Nevada Las Vegas in 2013 with a Bachelor of Science in Nursing. She devoted a decade to nursing across various specialties, including labor, delivery, postpartum, and hospice care. She became a Certified Lactation Counselor in 2017 and driven by her passion for travel, she became a Travel Specialist in 2022. In 2024, she transitioned to entrepreneurship in the financial industry alongside the travel and wellness industries. Her mission is to empower her community with their prenatal, travel, and financial well-being.

In her free time, she enjoys dancing and traveling, enriching her life with diverse experiences and creative pursuits.

Life is too short to settle for anything less than extraordinary, especially when it comes to living authentically as your true self.

Embracing Vulnerability:
The Courage to Live Your Best Life

By Ana Lucia Martinez, RN

"I'm scared. I have not been thinking. I messed up. I just had to communicate. I'm in Cancun alone and without the time, phone, money, ID, and passport. I want to go home. God, universe, and ancestors let me board my flight tomorrow."

That was my plea in Cancun, Mexico, after I lost my phone, money, ID, and passport when traveling in Cancun alone. It was not the fault of traveling alone. It was also not the fault of the city of Cancun. I had gotten careless in Coco Bongo and lost my fanny pack with all my important belongings. The days spent after losing everything were the scariest of them all. I was in a foreign country. As a travel agent, I felt embarrassed. I felt lost and lonely. I was enjoying my time alone traveling solo until I had zero connection with the people I loved. I didn't even have the time as my smartwatch was dead. My external charger was also lost. I don't know what I was thinking. I wasn't thinking. I let my guard down and made terrible decisions. My stress and anxiety levels were ten plus out of ten.

I had to keep grounding myself. Breathe in for two seconds and exhale for four or more seconds. I kept thinking if I should just give up now or keep going. I ended up calling my family from the hotel lobby at no charge and hearing my partner's and girls' voices helped me keep going. Yet, I felt so hopeless, not knowing if I was going to be able to go home or not. Thus, these are the steps I took:

Step 1: Asked the hotel what to do. I was aware I had to reach the embassy. However, the hotel told me to go to the police and make a report.

Step 2: Asked the hotel for a copy of my ID that they made when I checked in.

TIP: Have the hotel make a copy of your ID AND passport too or make copies at home and bring them. (I had felt so confident I would be able to access my Gmail and Google Drive, not thinking I would also lose my phone and then get myself locked out of it that I didn't make a copy. I had changed my password six days prior and activated two-step verification for the first time. I had forgotten my new password and didn't have my phone for the two-step verification.)

Step 3: Made the police report.

Step 4: Went to the embassy and reported my passport stolen. They gave me a piece of paper stating that the airline needed to call the Joint Security Program (JSP) or Customs and Border Protection (CBP), but it was up to the airline to let me board the flight.

Once the police report was completed and I had a copy of my ID, I called the banks and reported my cards lost and ordered replacements. Luckily, there had been no fraudulent charges.

Now, what else was there to do, but try to enjoy the rest of my last day in Cancun? I cried for some time in my hotel room and started repeating:

- I am worthy.
- I am worthy despite my mistakes.
- I am worthy of a life of peace and abundance.

I also started journaling. I was having a mandatory digital detox and what else was there to do? I wrote down my feelings, prayers, and positive affirmations. When I prayed, I prayed to go home. I finally was calm enough to go to the beach.

Once at the beach, I enjoyed the warmth of the ocean water, the warmth of the sun hitting my shoulders, and the sea breeze as it blew on my face. I cried silent tears hoping that I would be able to go home. I had not ever been that scared, not during my divorce or when my mom died. I felt stuck and it was my fault. I went to Cancun to reflect. My partner and I were undergoing a rough patch in our relationship and were originally going to go to Cancun as a couple. Yet, after everything was said and done, I ended up going alone and reflecting, I did.

After swimming in the ocean, I was able to calm down and take a nap on the beach chair. Hearing the ocean waves, feeling the sun on my skin, and feeling OK for a second in time. Oh, how I wished to turn back time! What was I thinking? I wasn't thinking... All I could hope for was that the prepaid taxi back to the airport would arrive on time the next day and that the airline, Frontier, would let me fly home.

As the next day came and went, I was happy to report that the taxi was early and waiting for me. Oh, it was one less thing to worry about! I felt a sense of relief off my shoulders. Next, at the airport, I was able to get through the airline counter. Thank God and the universe! Frontier called the necessary people and the supervisor at the counter let me pass. I felt a sense of relief. Next, I was able to go through security and she, too, let me pass showing my police report and photocopy of my ID. I felt a sense of relief. Lastly, I was getting to board the plane. My flight was delayed for one hour and the agent at the gate let me pass after verifying my identity with the supervisor at the counter. I was so relieved once I sat on my assigned seat on the plane. I was going home!

But...the flight kept getting delayed. We sat on the plane for three hours! Excuse after excuse was made until the pilot's time maxed out and was unable to fly. We then had to wait for all the luggage to be removed from the plane and wait for the canceled flight email to come through. I immediately got in line to talk to the agent at the gate. I didn't have a phone and what else could I do? I don't remember seeing courtesy phones in the Cancun airport. Luckily, seeing how distressed

I was, a fellow passenger let me borrow her phone. I was able to call my partner and let him know the flight had been canceled and Frontier was getting us a hotel for the night. By the time all was said and done, going through customs again, and getting checked into the hotel, it was midnight just to be picked up at 4 am for our 7 am flight. The passenger I roomed in with let me borrow her iPad and phone and I was able to book a flight home because Frontier would only provide the flight from Cancun to Dallas because I had requested to be on the 7 am flight and not the complimentary flight from Cancun to Ohio and Ohio to Las Vegas. What was I going to do in Ohio? It was so far from home and if I had a passport, I would not have minded. Thus, the need to buy my connecting flight from Dallas to Las Vegas.

The next morning, I once again had to go through every checkpoint and explain my unique situation…again! In a nutshell, our 7 am flight took off and I made it to Dallas. However, the next challenge began once we landed. Our flight landed on the tarmac and we had to take a bus to the gate. The bus drove us to the gate and kept us on the bus for approximately 15 minutes. As soon as those doors opened, I was able to take the stairs and rush to Customs. Without a passport, I had to talk to an agent who let me pass. I was so relieved! Yet, my flight, which was slightly delayed to begin with, landed in terminal D and I had to go to terminal E via the Skylink monorail, and to do that I had to go through TSA. The first security checkpoint took what felt like an eternity as I had limited time to reach my connecting flight. Once I reached the TSA agent, she had to get a supervisor who wanted a second piece of ID, which I did not have. I was told to buy another flight. That is when I couldn't help but cry out of the anxiety I felt at thinking I was stuck in Dallas. I left that security checkpoint and was walking away when I walked upon another security checkpoint and saw it had no one in line. I figured I would try my luck there. Once again, the TSA agent had to call a supervisor who wanted a second piece of ID. This time, I remembered I had my *HowMoneyWorks: Stop Being A*

Sucker book on me that had a picture of me on the inside page. The TSA supervisor let me pass! I was so grateful, I even hugged him! Yet, my backpack had to be checked thoroughly, and more time passed. Making it short, I missed my flight by a few minutes. They had closed the door and the Frontier worker wouldn't let me in. The plane was still there and seconds prior they allowed a Spirit steward in. I was so desperate to go home I even asked for mercy and offered him $100 (the passenger in Cancun had overheard my conversation and gave me $100 in case I needed it). After much crying, I was able to see there were American Airlines flights leaving out of terminal D and I figured maybe the agents at that flight gate could help me and they did. I was able to find the American Airlines customer service desk and use the airport's courtesy phone to call my partner to help me buy my flight home. The customer service desk then was able to print me my boarding pass.

At last, I was home! After two days of being in airports, experiencing flight delays, and the anxiety of being let into the US without a passport, I was home! There was no better feeling than coming home and reconciling with my partner, my knight in shining armor. It was an act of love to help me after how we had left our relationship. I was in a vulnerable situation and he helped me in my darkest moment.

What did I learn from this experience?

As women, we are taught to be strong, independent women. We are told we need to do everything like men, but we are biologically different. We cannot deny that our composition of hormones, muscle mass, etc. is different. We are not taught how to ask for help or receive help gracefully. I found that this was not a problem until I became a mother. I found that it did not matter if I was a working mother or a stay-at-home mother, it was all too much to handle on my own. When we attempt to be strong, independent women, as mothers, we live in a survival mode and masculine energy. I may be wrong, but that was my experience as a mother of three and the upbringing I experienced.

As the years went by, it took a lot of counseling, support, and trial and error to figure out how to live a life true to myself, a life of peace and abundance, a soft life as Lisa Glamour on YouTube explains. Here are four steps that will be broken down and explained to help guide you through your journey to live a life true to yourself. These steps can be done in the order described, in the order you find easiest to work on, or can be worked on simultaneously. There is no wrong or right way.

Step One: Mindset: "Live like you're dying or die like you never lived" Myron Golden

I invite you to consider the idea of changing your mindset to: "Live like you're dying or die like you never lived" Myron Golden https://www.youtube.com/live/KQCCfiYq5h8?si=YHI10yVoiNdEp Cl8

Why? It gives us a sense of URGENCY and reminds us that life is SHORT. It is OK to make mistakes because it helps us learn.

We live in a society that teaches us to be perfect, get straight 'A's to be worthy and that quitting or failure is not an option. How are we to learn if we do not try? How are we to see what works or not if we are afraid of failure, to be vulnerable? Working as a hospice nurse, I can attest that we take our life for granted. We believe we have all the time in the world. We put our dreams on the back burner and let our doubts and fears run our lives. We live in the future or the past. It is time to live in the present and savor every moment we can, except for 3 am blowouts if you are a mom. In *Sensual Symphony*, I go more into detail about mindset and write about letting go of negative beliefs, embracing a positive self-concept/image of yourself, social media, healing from past trauma, gaining financial independence, using your imagination, and learning the maybe; this or better philosophy. For this chapter, I have room to discuss financial independence.

Financial Independence

I believe that without a goal to become financially independent, it will be more challenging to live a life true to yourself. When there is a lack of financial security, we cannot do what we really want to do with our lives. We have a desperate energy and will usually make mistakes along the way like taking any job, even if it is a job you do not like or making bad financial decisions that makes us go into debt and slaves to credit card companies.

So, what does becoming financially independent mean? It is a work-optional lifestyle that still meets expenses and _____ (you fill in the blank/what is your ideal life?).

How are you going to gain financial independence? You will need a financial roadmap. Check out: HowMoneyWorks – howmoneyworks .com/anam. In a nutshell, there are seven money milestones:

1. Financial Education
2. Proper Protection
3. Emergency Fund
4. Debt Management
5. Cash Flow
6. Build Wealth
7. Protect Wealth

Next, you need to figure out what you want. If you don't know what you want, read *Rich As F*ck: More Money Than You Know What To Do With* by Amanda Frances. It is a life-changing book. My hope would be that you figure out what you want.

FYI: This step takes time. Without it, you do not have the freedom to live your best life. For me, it took the trip to Cancun to finally help me prioritize my finances, reduce my debts, and stop spending on so many trips that I could not afford when trying to live within my means. For so long I was so afraid that I would die young like my mom who died at the young age of 53. It was a self-limiting belief, a belief I finally was able to let go..

Step Two: The Heart

We all have trauma that we need to process by acknowledging our feelings which can be uncomfortable. We need to be able to feel our feelings, yet not become those feelings. That is where receiving counseling and going to therapy comes into play. When we heal ourselves, we are able to move forward, and then we are able to know what we want and know ourselves. You will be able to prioritize yourself without feeling guilty. Otherwise, we keep neglecting ourselves, being people pleasers, putting others first, and becoming resentful. We need to learn to say "no" and set boundaries.

A daily practice I was recommended was journaling and answering two questions daily:

1. What was one thing I did for myself today?
2. What am I proud of today?

These two questions are short yet profound. They help you realize if you are putting yourself first or not. Because our emotions are powerful and we need to release them one way or another, journaling is a great way to channel those emotions and release them. The next step is to communicate what you want. You need to be able to be true to yourself, analyze yourself, and voice to yourself, your partner, your kids, and a higher power what you want. Self-care is not selfish. It is self-love. Treat yourself, you deserve it.

Step 3: The Soul

Whether you are religious or spiritual, whether you believe in God, another higher power, or the universe, we all look up to a power outside of us. Having a strong faith practice helps ground and center ourselves. Our soul wants and/or needs to express gratitude for the things we already have and learn to WANT the things we already have. For me, learning to WANT the things I already had was a game changer and helped me keep a positive mindset and perspective. Here are some affirmations that help with the soul. Fill in the underlined words with your own words:

1. I know it will all work out.
2. I trust in <u>the higher power</u>.
3. <u>The universe</u> always has my back.

Step Four: The Body: Get Comfortable In Your Own Skin

Our body is a temple. It is the vehicle in which we explore and experience the world. Living a healthy lifestyle is key to having quality of life. For me, that means having the ability to be independent of my activities of daily living. It is something that is in my control.

What does living a healthy lifestyle entail?

- Physical Relaxation - work with your body, not against it
  - o Tense/relax, progressive relaxation
  - o Massages
  - o Chiropractor
  - o Urinate often
  - o Freedom to move, drink, eat
- Physical activity (ex: walking, exercising, hiking, dancing, joining a gym)
- Nutrition (well-rounded diet, moderation, supplements, Herbally Grounded at herballygrounded.com)
- Hygiene (routines and natural products, for example, no aluminum deodorants)
  - o Natural products (for example, DoTERRA)

If becoming financially independent is already a goal you are working on, it will make it easier to accomplish the activities recommended. Next, the more you decide to prioritize your body, the more you will begin to feel good in your own skin and have quality of life. In my personal experience, dancing was my lifesaver. At first, it was awkward and I felt vulnerable. Over time, like any skill, I began to feel confident and I was having fun and working out. The more types of dances I tried, the more I learned, and the more comfortable I felt in my own skin. I was able to touch my body and feel confident doing so. As a Certified Lactation Counselor, I have been surprised on more than one occasion how many women do not feel comfortable touching their breasts to monitor their breast tissue which is essential to avoid any breast clogs or worse, mastitis (an infection of the breast tissue). In *Sensual Symphony*, I also discuss how your environment is important, how you dress and routine matter, and recommend boudoir photography to help feel empowered.

Conclusion

Living a life true to yourself is a vulnerable journey that evolves over time and that is perfectly fine. Our dreams change, our goals change. My life experiences and working as a hospice nurse and travel agent have shown me what is truly important to me. Our life experiences are like a roller coaster with many ups and downs and in your rock-bottom vulnerable moments, you can choose to get back up. It is never too late to change and make different decisions. Looking back, I made a rookie mistake. Had I bought travel insurance, I would have saved myself so much mental and emotional distress! You live and learn. I am here to help dear readers!

Erin LoPorto

Embodied Freedom Life Coaching
Certified Yoga Therapist, Health & Life Coach,
Energy Healer and Speaker

https://www.linkedin.com/in/erinloporto/
https://www.facebook.com/erinloporto.yoga
https://www.instagram.com/erinloporto/
https://erinloporto.com/

Erin LoPorto is the founder of Embodied Freedom Life Coaching and the creator of the transformative "Embody, Empower, Evolve" formula, dedicated to healing trauma, eating disorders, and fostering personal growth. Introduced to yoga in 2001 at the Savannah College of Art and Design, Erin has since embarked on a profound journey of healing and self-discovery through the 8-limbed path of yoga.

With extensive training—including a two-year internship at Kripalu Center for Yoga and Health—she has become a certified expert in Kripalu Yoga, PranaFlow, and TriYoga Therapy, amassing over 1,000 hours of Yoga Therapy training. Erin is also a skilled bodyworker, certified in Reiki and Thai Yoga Massage.

Based in Acton, MA, Erin teaches yoga at Walden Behavioral Care and

Revolution Community Yoga. Her playful, intuitive approach empowers clients to achieve physical and spiritual renewal. Outside of work, she enjoys exploring New England's natural beauty and engaging in personal growth and social justice initiatives.

From Body Hate to Body Love

By Erin LoPorto

It was many years ago when I showed up at a therapist's office early one day. She was helping me with an eating disorder that I had struggled with for almost a decade. I feared I was killing myself with my behavior. Which is why I was shocked and outraged to see my therapist chain-smoking before our session. How could she help me when she had a habit that was slowly killing her too?

I left that day convinced that there were no heroes and determined that if I were going to heal – I was going to have to do it myself. I made a U-turn on the way home that day and drove myself to the library. I took out every book I could on personal development, eating disorders, and addiction.

Within 10 weeks I had experienced a complete transformation – physically, emotionally, and spiritually. And I self-healed what I had been struggling with for a decade. I taught myself to love and respect myself. I know what love and respect feel like now.

It's been over 20 years since I moved begyond recovery and into that newfound freedom to be me – no matter what shape, size, or presentation is present that day. I no longer subscribe to the shoulds and supposed-to's ascribed by culture media and industry. Even as my weight, my lifestyle, my health, and my ambitions have gone through many changes… I have consistently held myself in the lens that I am good enough, I have much to offer and that beauty is in the eye of the beholder.

I have not participated in a single diet for the purpose of weight loss and I have not spent a single day hating myself or some part of me even though I have aged and experienced changes in weight, shape, tone, and capacity. My body is a great friend, resource, and partner in this life – that I love and protect – unconditionally.

And since I know very few other people who can also say that – I feel compelled to share my story and my method for the purpose of liberating others from the frustration and exhaustion of chronic dieting or the hell of living with an eating disorder or in constant dissatisfaction or hate of oneself.

I remember that hate. I remember abusing my body in a variety of ways before terms like self-harm were common vernacular. I remember feeling like my body was constantly betraying me. I hated the fact that I had a body. I fantasized about making it disappear or someday beating it into submission. I longed to be free of it.

I remember looking at myself in the mirror the first time I decided to see my body differently. What if I had been looking at my body all wrong? It wasn't against me. It wasn't betraying me. I was against it. If anything, I had betrayed it. And even so, my body, showed up every day to serve me with everything it had.

It was hard to acknowledge, but my body experienced every hurt and hardship I experienced. It began to occur to me that I didn't hate my body because it was bad. I hated my body because it was carrying for me, everything I wanted to forget.

Instead of seeing my body as fat or broken, I began to get curious about what unresolved story it was holding for me. I started to thank it for carrying all the things I didn't want to even think about. I started appreciating my body's patience – and honesty. No matter how many others I could convince I was fine – my body was there to remind me that some parts weren't.

No matter how many situations I could outrun – I couldn't outrun my body. And as it stared back at me with all its imperfections – I could feel that it had far less judgement of me than I had for it. In fact, I could feel my body's determination that no matter what happened to me, or what I did to it… my body was going to do everything in its power to thrive anyway.

And so I cried for my body and myself. For the two of us. Both so alone – unable to see that we were together and needing each other. I decided I was going to love my body no matter what – the same way it had been trying to love all of me – even the parts I didn't know how to love.

I began to touch my collarbone and shoulder. I could appreciate that part that made me feel strong. I touched my stomach – and remembered wearing a two-piece bathing suit as a kid loving how warm my belly got in the sun. I remembered that I didn't always hate my body. I once had fun in my body. Running through the yard pretending I was a horse, playing on the swing set pretending I was an Olympic gymnast, choreographing dance routines pretending I was a famous singer.

And so in the mirror – day by day – I began to dance and move and reclaim every square inch of my body. I began to appreciate the features of my family that were passed down – and I worked to make them feel like mine. I began to understand the ways my body bulked up for protection, called out with sensation to warn me about people and situations, and hurt to let me know it needed rest or a different kind of support.

I realized that I owed my body for my life and that it delivered on giving me life every single day. Some days were easier than others to find appreciation for my body – but I had dropped all other options. I was determined to find the way. And I knew from a decade of trying – I could not hate my way to loving myself. And that if I could love my body at its worst – it would be easy to love at its best. Loving myself in all my states was the only thing I imagined could free me from the body war I had been engaged with for so long.

But it wasn't just my body I needed to look at. I had very little understanding of why I did what I did with food or why. It was one thing to work towards appreciating myself in the mirror but it was another thing to try to manage the compulsions I had around food. And so I started telling myself to "slow down." A hundred times a day I would repeat that phrase to myself. I knew I needed to think and move slower to see myself clearly.

I have since learned the Sanskrit word "samskara," which means "knot." It refers to the place in the body where life's impressions get tied together creating sensations, reactions, and shortcuts in the body and mind. Different from the psychological term trigger which refers to the outer circumstance, samskara refers to the inner experience – the place the charge lives.

Life had always seemed out of control. I always felt like life or the people in it were making me do things that I regretted.

The words "slow down" became my mantra. It allowed me to see and feel and to untie the knots that I had with my relationship with food, myself, and everything else in the world. I began to recognize the thought patterns that were strung together. The outer circumstances were not what made me act in ways I regretted as it had always seemed. The 3rd, 4th, 5th, or 6th thought in response was what caused me to act… and every other thought before that was an opportunity to choose differently.

The more I slowed down the more off-ramps and choices I could see.

I also started to learn so much about myself. I shifted out of people-pleasing and started making the choices that felt good and right to me. I started to learn about other things that could soothe me or give me strength. I started trusting that I could handle the hard feelings.

The first few times the feelings would come, it was overwhelming. I felt like my skin was crawling, like thunder was in my stomach; it felt like the only way out would be to tear my skin off. Before this time in my life, I was prone to having a temper and panic attacks. Both created a discharge that would relieve some of those torturous sensations.

As I worked with my mantra, instead of moving away from the feelings – I practiced staying with them. Sometimes I would moan, cry, or breathe deeply. But I learned that the feeling would always pass on its own – I learned to be there with my body and for my body no matter what. With those simple words "slow down" I learned that I could hold myself through anything. I started to heal the traumas my body remembered. I started to become fearless.

There was a 3-mile loop near my house. I committed to walking it every day. Sometimes, I would do that loop in under 45 minutes. Sometimes, the same path would take me well over an hour as my body dragged. Sometimes, I walked at 2 am with a slight buzz after coming home from the bar.

For the first time, I wasn't holding movement as a calorie-burning contest. I was using this walk to witness myself and build trust and understanding for myself. Every time I walked, I listened to my thoughts, felt my sensations – and built an even stronger relationship with myself. As my past unfolded, the many voices in my head diminished until there was one – my voice. A part of myself that I feared was gone forever was actually okay – and filled with as much wisdom, energy, and love as ever.

My body communicated to me through sensation and energy. I learned that many of the things I thought were good for it – didn't serve me well. When I followed the rules of diet culture, my body would often struggle on our walk. Other times when I thought I was "so bad" because I had over-indulged in something – my body seemed to appreciate it. I would notice an extra spring in my step.

My reactivity slowed – and rather than stop at the first sign of pain or feeling out of breath, I would kindly say, "It's okay, pain, you are welcome here." The pain and discomfort that would previously have stopped me would often dissipate like magic. Other times it would stay or increase… I would continue to engage with it, changing my stride to see if I could support my knee, hip, or ankle more. Sometimes, I would stop and stretch something and start again.

I learned to have a direct relationship with pain and discomfort. I began to understand that every sensation is a communication from the body. By responding I could engage in conversation with it. And I learned to discern and decipher all sorts of different messages as I learned to move with more grace, ease, and presence than I had ever known.

The highs and lows in my moods began to balance out. I had a list that I carried with me of things I loved and loved to do. I kept adding to that list and when I would feel low, I would pull out that list and choose something to do to shift my energy. I learned to stop forcing everything.

When my body said yes to something – it would provide me with more energy and when it said no, it would drain my energy. I learned to trust my body's rhythm and my body's desires. I also learned how to get all my have-to's done in kinder ways that incorporated my body's preferences and energy.

I also journaled as a way to honor the things I was realizing about myself. It was almost like I was writing a manual about who I am and how I operate. And the more I learned the more I loved and appreciated myself. I was able to let go of the many unfair expectations and attachments I had to false versions of myself.

I was able to be present and free in the moment. Standing for myself and taking chances the former me never would have been able to. The former me was always on the verge of emotional flooding, quiet desperation, and a need to flee. The new me had discovered patience and kindness for myself that looked like fearlessness and felt like freedom.

I was lucky to be in art school, studying media and honing a craft that gave me so many outlets for expression. Studying media for classes also gifted me space and awareness to recognize the manipulations in messages to serve industry rather than individuals. I was able to stop internalizing the messages designed to sell something and learned to think and develop my own values to live by.

Many of my assignments allowed me to share my story directly or abstractly. In life drawing classes, I learned that beauty was in the eye of the beholder – and I learned to see the stories in every body. The more I could love and appreciate the quirks of every body the more I could appreciate my own. The more I could appreciate my own body the less I found myself comparing or judging myself with everyone else. I learned to see the beauty and be excited by diversity in myself and others. I no longer tried to win by conforming.

The fact is, most of us learned from a young age not to trust ourselves. Whether it was a parent, teacher, or priest we learned to look to an outside authority to tell us what's right and wrong, to tell us what to do. We were taught to hold our bodies and voices still in classes – affirming that the body by nature is wrong and must be controlled.

When nobody is feeling right in themselves, it's no wonder that sexism, racism, ableism, fatphobia, and so much hate thrive in our world, that 80% of the US population reports being dissatisfied with their bodies and that we blindly trust and pay billion-dollar industries to tell us what to do with our bodies without considering the feedback our bodies give back. And to help us feel better "self-care" is sold in the same cookie-cutter way drugs, diets, and everything else are sold – a promise of happily ever after.

In my experience – we can't offer ourselves "self-care" if we don't know ourselves deeply – if we haven't built the practice of listening to and trusting ourselves. Real self-care results in us loving and appreciating ourselves more and the effects are permanent.

Today, I help people rebuild their relationship with their body and self so that they heal traumas and expectations and create their greatest mental and physical health and personal expression based on their own value system. I built off of everything I learned about myself in that 10-week period so many years ago, and everything I continued to study I became a yoga therapist, energy healer, bodyworker, and life and health coach. I have trained my eyes to see the beauty in everyone – and can reflect back an unconditional love and appreciation that most have never known.

I believe that most of the challenges we face in this world are a result of the lack of relationships we have with ourselves. As we hold ourselves to unfair expectations – we automatically resent or hold others to the same unfair expectations. As we reject and fear parts of ourselves, we reject and fear those same parts in others – even when they show up in the face of our lover or child. And as we ask more of ourselves than we have to give, we don't think twice about taking from our planet the resources she can't replenish.

I believe that truly knowing and loving ourselves and the bodies that carry us allows for a better world and connects us to our own humanity. Beyond the concepts of right or wrong is simply the truth of what is – holding a mirror up and challenging us to make room for the infinite potential within each and all of us. As we can only love what we understand, I believe it's time we all "slow down" and take the time to understand ourselves so we can better understand others so that we can have more love and peace in this world.

Alexandra Christ

Unstoppable You Coaching
Peak Performance Mindset Coach and Speaker

https://www.linkedin.com/in/alexandrachrist/
https://www.instagram.com/aliganoush/
https://attractwell.com/AlexandraChrist
https://www.tiktok.com/@alwaysliveextraordinary

As a peak performance mindset coach, Alexandra loves helping people tap into their full potential and manifest their biggest dreams. She's all about breaking through those sneaky limiting beliefs that hold you back from the life you know you're meant for—more joy, love, wealth, and success.

Alexandra knows what it feels like to be burned out and stuck in a rut—that's why she loves helping people, because she's been there too. She teaches using humor and joy, believing you can have fun in every moment. People often say Alexandra is magic, but she's simply living what she teaches and has manifested incredible dreams herself. Feeling stuck even though you know what to do? She'll help you ditch the self-doubt, stress less, and step confidently into the life you deserve. She can't wait to celebrate your wins as you embrace your passions and create a life full of exciting possibilities!

Manifesting 101—
Your Blueprint to Abundance

By Alexandra Christ

For twenty years, I slogged through the corporate grind, enjoying the security of a regular paycheck. On the outside, everything seemed fine, but inside I was a mess. Every morning, a knot of dread tightened in my stomach, signaling something was seriously wrong. Burnout had become my constant companion. The once-exciting career had turned into a monotonous grind, and I began to resent every minute at my desk. My colleagues, who used to be my support system, started excluding me from happy hours, making me feel like an outsider. The team dynamic shifted from camaraderie to conflict, leaving me more isolated than ever.

As burnout intensified, so did my anger and frustration. I hated how much time I spent at work, feeling trapped and powerless. One question haunted me: If today were my last day, would I have lived a great life? The answer was a resounding no. Deep down, I knew I had more to offer, yet here I was, stuck and unfulfilled. But what could I do? I needed that paycheck. I felt paralyzed and numb. Desperate for clarity, I booked a massage, hoping to unknot the stress. As I lay there, I whispered a plea to the universe: "What do I do? I want to change my life, but I don't know how. I want to live with freedom and joy and make a bigger impact, but how?" The answer came softly: Do nothing. It will be taken care of.

Seriously? Do nothing? I needed a clear plan, not some vague message. Frustrated and exhausted, I drifted off to sleep on the massage table, feeling more uncertain than ever. The following weekend, my boyfriend and I discussed starting a family. I had frozen my eggs, hoping to use them with the right partner. We spent time with his family, dreaming about our future together. That night, my phone rang with an unidentified number. The message was devastating: my fertility doctor informed me that an accident at the storage facility had destroyed my eggs. At that moment, the world stopped. The dream of becoming a mother, which I had nurtured for so long, was shattered in an instant. The loss was indescribable, a deep, aching void that swallowed me whole.

I broke the news to my boyfriend, who initially tried to comfort me. But the next day, his demeanor changed. He seemed nervous, avoiding eye contact. That night, after a trip to the gym, he said the dreaded words: "We need to talk." Every alarm bell went off in my head. I could feel an emptiness in my chest and a sinking feeling in my stomach. He told me he no longer wanted to be with me. Tears flowed heavily, blurring my vision. I was struggling to catch my breath. Saying I was in shock was an understatement. Desperate for an explanation, I asked, "Is this because of the fertility news?" He was silent, then muttered: "Um," shook his head, got up, walked to the door, and said, "Goodbye."

The next day, I dragged myself to work, feeling like a ghost. The combined weight of losing my fertility and my relationship in 24 hours was unbearable. A friend called to say a pillar of our music community had died unexpectedly, and I felt like my soul couldn't handle one more ounce of grief. My body, already battered by stress, was on the brink of collapse. My manager let me work from home for a couple of days, but this was a privilege only afforded to me—not my team. When I returned, upper management threatened to take my vacation days because of company policy, even though I had completed all my work. I felt like a prisoner with no rights. I left to see my doctor and poured out everything: The boyfriend leaving, the friend's death, the disaster with the eggs, and the toxic environment at work.

Good fortune struck when my doctor authorized a one-month stress leave because I didn't have the tools to deal with so much grief all at once. Tension at work was growing. No one knew why I was gone or what was going on with me and that became a source of contention over the following months. And then it happened. I got called into a room with my boss, my manager, and the manager's boss. The alarm bells I had felt on my couch returned, and my biggest fear came true—my services were no longer needed. "Take your time cleaning out your desk, but it must be completed by tonight." I was stunned.

That first Monday without a job, I went to the beach. I wanted to ground myself and clear my mind. As I sat there, I realized I had actually created the scenario of getting fired. My discontent was so strong that I constantly visualized a life outside the office; one where I could impact others on a much bigger scale. So, I wrote down everything I learned and got clear about what I truly wanted.

You Don't Get What You Want, You Get Who You Are

As I reflected, I realized I had been a disgruntled worker bee attracting negative interactions. Deep down, I wanted to be my own boss. To make that happen, I had to change how I saw myself. I knew that self-image is the guiding compass to what you get in life, sort of like autopilot on an airplane. If the plane goes off course, the autopilot makes corrections to bring it back. I was at a turning point: I could stay put and let auto-pilot keep me feeling stuck and dissatisfied or I could bust out of this mold and attempt to steer the plane somewhere more to my liking. I had my work cut out for myself.

Given I had been let go, I now needed to think about how I wanted to feel in my new scenario, to question my dominating thoughts. I couldn't allow myself to think: "This will never happen to me," or "I have the worst luck," because those thoughts put up a big wall of resistance. I'd actually repel what I wanted. I needed to think and act like a successful CEO, not like a minimum-wage minion. These mindsets are like different radio stations—they broadcast completely different tunes.

I started using my imagination to create a life of freedom and joy, quite the opposite of the frustrating energy that had permeated my life. What would that freedom and joy feel like? I sat in my imagination, tuning into all my senses, and began to envision my ideal life. First I had to get past my present work feelings. When I thought of work, my posture slumped, my thoughts were filled with doubt and my actions (or lack thereof) reflected that belief. Until then, this self-image had set the tone of my life. I had to create a new picture and feeling inside of myself to identify with.

If Thoughts and Feelings Can Get Me Fired, They Can Also Create the Life I Want

I needed to get really clear on what I wanted: To have the freedom to do as I wished at the time of my choosing. Say my parents suggested an impromptu lunch, I would be able to drop everything and enjoy that time with them without having to beg for coverage. If I felt like moving to a tiny village in Greece by the sea, I would go. When friends needed emotional support, I now had the flexibility to hop on a plane and be there for them without worrying about my job.

And guess what? I made it all happen. I got crystal clear on my desires, wrote them down, took action and circumstances presented themselves to materialize that lifestyle. I saw myself waking up every morning excited, smiling, and full of energy. I felt confident and capable, standing naturally taller. I saw my body language exuding assurance, and feeling empowered. I pictured myself working with amazing people, helping them achieve their dreams, and ending sessions with a celebration dance. I felt the warmth of the sun on my face as I traveled to beautiful places. I heard the laughter of friends and family around me. I smelled the fresh ocean air as I walked along the beach and imagined wiping the sand from between my toes. I tasted the sweetness of freedom and the joy of living a purposeful life.

And to change my life, I began making decisions from my desired end result, and not from my limiting current circumstances.

Identify Limiting Beliefs to Remove Mental Blocks

Let's talk about those pesky limiting beliefs that have held me trapped in an unfulfilling job all those years. These are the sneaky little thoughts that can hold us back, without us even realizing it. Common limiting beliefs can include: "I'm not good enough," "I don't deserve success," "Money is hard to come by," "I'll never find love," or "I'm too old to change my career." These beliefs are like invisible chains that keep us stuck in the same place, unable to move forward. I have realized that these types of beliefs create a self-fulfilling prophecy, making it almost impossible to break free and achieve goals.

For example, if I believe "I'm not good enough," I might shy away from opportunities that could lead me to success because deep down, I might not think I deserve them. Or if "Money is hard to come by," I could sabotage my financial success by abandoning pursuing higher-paying jobs or managing my money poorly.

I realized that *if my thoughts could get me fired, they could also create the life I wanted.* So I dove into personal development and spirituality, going on journeys with shamans and doing the inner work. I worked with various mentors, and when I discovered Bob Proctor, his teachings resonated with me deeply. I joined his inner circle to learn how he thinks, what he reads, and what he believes, absorbing everything like a sponge. I became a consultant for Bob and now I get to teach his material and change lives. But here's the thing: I had to *take action*. I found him, enrolled to study with him, and went into business with him. Now, I use these principles to guide others to live extraordinary lives.

Rewriting Your Story

Rewriting your story starts with recognizing these limiting beliefs and then consciously replacing them with empowering ones. It's about changing the narrative you tell yourself.

When you get crystal clear on your vision and focus on it daily, the universe begins to align circumstances and events to bring your desires to life. If you want a car, **be specific** so the universe knows exactly what to deliver. You don't want to end up with a toy car when you're dreaming of the real deal. It's all about having clarity, believing in your vision, and maintaining consistent focus. If you want to attract more money, you can't keep thinking, "I don't have money," because the universe will give you more lack and hit you with big bills.

Frequency and Vibration

Frequency and vibration: We hear these buzzwords all the time, but what do they really mean? Picture this: When I prefer something, I'm not in resistance. For example, I might prefer vanilla ice cream, but if the deli only has chocolate, I'm still cool with ordering chocolate. Insisting things must be in a certain way means I'm actually blocking what I want. So an open attitude keeps me in the flow. It's a preference, not a requirement.

You and I are constantly emitting a frequency, a vibration. When we are happy, joyful, and confident, our vibration is high and fast, making it easier to attract what we want. On the flip side, when we're negative, sad, or unconfident, our vibration is low and slow, making it harder to attract what we desire.

We're always vibrating, and our frequency changes with our mood. You attract faster from a joy vibration, so I encourage my clients to have fun while they transform.

I wrote out my preferences for how I wanted to live, feel, and what my ideal life would look like. I fantasized about living on an island in Greece, coaching from my laptop. If it didn't happen, I'd be okay. I knew this because I was content in the moment of using my imagination to dream.

I realized that if millions of dollars didn't magically appear in my bank account, I'd still be fine, and this took all the pressure off. I started operating from a place of ease, joy, and flow, regularly asking myself, "What would I love?" I had so much fun daydreaming, seeing myself as the main character in my story. At first, I saw myself on the screen of the movie in my mind, then *I stepped into* the movie and could see my manicured hands as I gave a client a high-five. When you see yourself on the screen, you're disassociated, but when you're actually in the scene, seeing your hands and feet, you're living in the end result.

How to Channel Your Inner Badass and Embody the New, Unstoppable You:

The same old you will get the same old results

To start, pick a trigger to remind you of your new identity. For me, it was brushing my teeth. I switched to brushing with my left hand to create new neural pathways, staring into my own eyes in the mirror, smiling back, and playing the movie of my ideal life in my mind. Every time I saw a mirror or thought about brushing my teeth, I anchored myself to this exciting new version, having a blast with the thrill of my fantastic preference.

Next, while still looking in the mirror, I focused on my body posture. I tightened my abs, stood tall with my shoulders back, and became her—the successful, confident coach who loves her life and helps others elevate. I made sure my head was held high, my eyes were bright, and my smile was wide.

Later, as I walked down the street, I walked as her. Anytime I tightened my core and pulled my shoulders back, I reminded myself: Be her now. I lived as her, from the end result.

Embodying a new version of yourself involves your thoughts, feelings, and biology. The same old you will get the same old results, so this step is crucial. Be the version you want to be now. Be grateful that you have it (gratitude is a high vibe), celebrate how wonderful each day is, and know that it is all coming together!

The Secret Sauce: Feeling and Visualizing Your End Result

Here's the secret sauce: You tap into the feeling of the experience. Trust me, when you get into the feeling of joy and excitement, you're sending out a high-vibe frequency that attracts what you want. I saw myself living a lifestyle of freedom, and guess what? I attracted Bob Proctor into my life, and his work became the vehicle for my internal shifts, allowing me to help others too!

It's not just about thinking positively or repeating affirmations—it's about genuinely feeling as if you already have what you desire. This makes all the difference.

If you're dreaming of a new job that excites and fulfills you, don't just think about it; feel it. Picture yourself waking up in the morning, excited to start your day. Feel the joy and satisfaction as you walk into your new office, or even as you work from home in a job that allows you flexibility. Hear the sounds around you, see the environment in vivid detail, and most importantly, feel the emotions as if they are happening right now.

When you visualize the end result, you're not just daydreaming; you're creating a new reality in your mind. Your brain can't distinguish between what's vividly imagined and what's real, so it starts to align your thoughts, actions, and energy with this new reality. This is where the magic happens.

Think about it like this: If you're visualizing a goal but you're feeling anxious or doubtful, you're sending mixed signals. But when you feel the joy, excitement, and gratitude as if you've already achieved it, you're tuning into the frequency of your desires. This alignment is what attracts your goals into your life.

Say you want to attract more money and abundance. Don't just think, "I want more money." Visualize the end result. See yourself enjoying financial freedom, paying off debts, and having plenty of savings. Feel the relief and excitement of being able to afford anything you need and desire. Imagine making purchases without worry, investing in your future, and even helping others with your wealth. The more you immerse yourself in these feelings, the more you align yourself with the reality you want to create.

In my case, I wanted out of the office grind and into a life of freedom— to do what I wanted when I wanted and to help others so we could win together.

I'm thrilled to share that I'm finishing this chapter while traveling around Europe on a one-way ticket. My old job never would've let me go for more than two weeks, and now I get to choose!

If I can create a life of time, money, and freedom, so can you! Sure, I might not have my babies, but these days I wake up light and happy, and no longer feel a knot in my stomach caused by the daily grind and the threat of burnout. And I get to guide others to live an extraordinary life through my mindset coaching.

Perhaps, I can help you too. If you're looking to dream big, feel deeply, and watch your vision become reality, why not schedule a discovery session, and let's get crystal clear on what you really want?

JOIN THE MOVEMENT!
#BAUW

Becoming An Unstoppable Woman
With She Rises Studios

She Rises Studios was founded by Hanna Olivas and Adriana Luna Carlos, the mother-daughter duo, in mid-2020 as they saw a need to help empower women worldwide. They are the podcast hosts of the *She Rises Studios Podcast* and Amazon best-selling authors and motivational speakers who travel the world. Hanna and Adriana are the movement creators of #BAUW - Becoming An Unstoppable Woman: The movement has been created to universally impact women of all ages, at whatever stage of life, to overcome insecurities, and adversities, and develop an unstoppable mindset. She Rises Studios educates, celebrates, and empowers women globally.

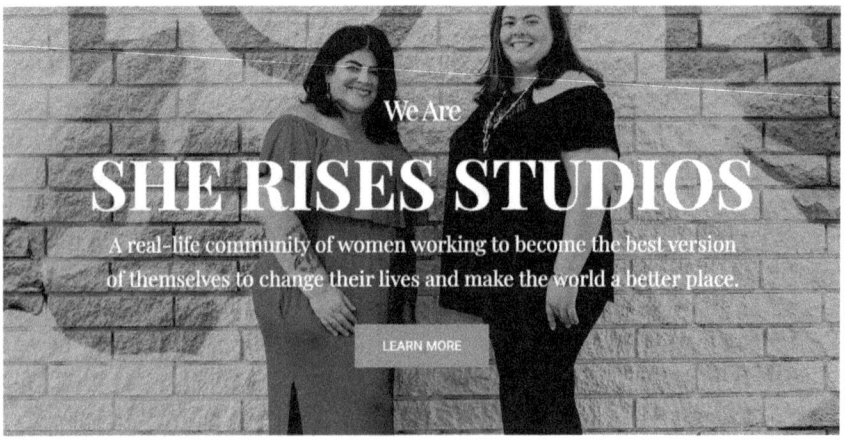

Looking to Join Us in our Next Anthology or Publish YOUR Own?

She Rises Studios Publishing offers full-service publishing, marketing, book tour, and campaign services. For more information, contact info@sherisesstudios.com

We are always looking for women who want to share their stories and expertise and feature their businesses on our podcasts, in our books, and in our magazines.

SEE WHAT WE DO

OUR PODCAST   **OUR BOOKS**   **OUR SERVICES**

Be featured in the Becoming An Unstoppable Woman magazine, published in 13 countries and sold in all major retailers. Get the visibility you need to LEVEL UP in your business!

Have your own TV show streamed across major platforms like Roku TV, Amazon Fire Stick, Apple TV and more!

Learn to leverage your expertise. Build your online presence and grow your audience with FENIX TV.
https://fenixtv.sherisesstudios.com/

Visit www.SheRisesStudios.com to see how YOU can join the #BAUW movement and help your community to achieve the UNSTOPPABLE mindset.

Have you checked out the *She Rises Studios Podcast?*

Find us on all MAJOR platforms: Spotify, IHeartRadio, Apple Podcasts, Google Podcasts, etc.

Looking to become a sponsor or build a partnership?

Email us at info@sherisesstudios.com

www.ingramcontent.com/pod-product-compliance
Lightning Source LLC
Chambersburg PA
CBHW071320120626
46546CB00002B/386